THE MOBILE BOARDROOM

Top tips for business success

Nik Askaroff & Julian Clay

Thorogood Publishing Ltd
10-12 Rivington Street
London EC2A 3DU
Telephone: 020 7749 4748

Email: info@thorogoodpublishing.co.uk
Web: www.thorogoodpublishing.co.uk

A CIP catalogue record for this book is available
from the British Library.

Paperback ISBN: (10) 1854188305 (13)
9781854188304

Ebook ISBN: (10) 1854188313 (13) 9781854188311

Printed and bound in Great Britain by
Marston Book Services Ltd, Oxfordshire

Table of Contents

Chapter 8

Mergers and acquisitions...............................137

Chapter 9

Management buy-outs...................................151

About the authors

Nik Askaroff FCA

Nik is the founder and CEO of EMC. He is a former President of the UK-based South Eastern Society of Chartered Accountants, past Chairman of both Business Link Sussex and Sussex Enterprise (the Chamber of Commerce for Sussex).

He holds board positions with six companies and at EMC focuses on strategy, team management, merger and acquisition work and commercial business development. He has considerable overseas experience, particularly in the emerging markets of China, Russia and India as well as the USA and most European countries.

Nik qualified as a Chartered Accountant in 1980. His first position in industry was in a small family fashion textile company. He also experienced at first hand the problems that can arise in second generation family businesses.

He has been involved in many projects ranging from chief executive of a listed electronics company to non-executive director for one of the country's leading freight forwarders. More recently he has been actively involved in the health sector, furnishing fabrics, engineering, ergonomic office equipment, construction and PR and marketing industries.

Julian Clay

Julian was a top sales performer and senior manager in Kodak's Office Imaging division. Since 1998 he has worked with a number of different types and size of company (from SMEs to 'Times Top 100'), to help develop and implement successful sales strategies.

His key strengths are to work with companies to increase sales in a number of different, competitive markets in order to achieve growth. This includes having a good sales process, coaching people in a sales role and working as an interim sales director. He has also written and delivered many sales development programmes.

His expertise lies in understanding the core business challenges that companies face as well as having the ability to assess and develop a sales team's skills. He has written a sales forecasting software programme to help companies manage their opportunities well and win more business.

Julian has an honours degree in Psychology and Business Studies and is the co-author of *The Sales Manager's Desktop Guide* and *Sales Strategy for Business Growth*, and author of *Successful Selling Solutions* (Thorogood publishers).

Thank you

The Mobile Boardroom had input from a number of EMC consultants. Special thanks go to those who wrote or who made a valuable contribution to the following chapters:

Chapter 1 – Better business planning – Giselle Barrowcliffe

Chapter 2 - Raising capital – Michael Pay

Chapter 3 - Financial management – Desmond High

Chapter 4 - Sales and marketing – Martin Stanton

Chapter 5 – Information technology – Jon Green

Chapter 8 - Mergers and acquisitions – Ryan Smith

Chapter 9 – Management buy-outs – Desmond High

Chapter 10 - Post-acquisition management – Michael Pay

Foreword

My parents were immigrants into the United Kingdom in the 1950s and they started their own business in 1956 in fashion textiles manufacturing and distribution. As one of six boys I was brought up on the factory floor surrounded by parcels and sewing machines. My first exhibition was at the age of six as a model and my first job for the company was as an export sales-man at the age of sixteen. My father was always concerned with what he didn't know but at the same time he made money from what he did know. He always said that it was the accountants that made all the money so at the age of eighteen I went off and qualified as a chartered accountant.

During the next fifteen years on a path from Finance Director to Chief Executive of a listed company I was always seeking out advice, looking at different ways of doing things and finding better solutions for what was being done. Often the shortest conversation led to the biggest benefit and I learned that it was important to retain people who had good ideas and could put these into action.

In 1989, after selling all my shares in one company, I set up EMC Management Consultants Ltd to provide advice to the Small and Medium Enterprise (SME) sector on whatever basis they could afford but most importantly for only as long as it provided real value. It was clear that the £2-£20 million annual revenue sector could not afford full-time top flight executives but were in desperate need of them in a more limited way on a regular basis. So it was then that we pioneered the concept of the 'mobile boardroom'.

EMC only uses proven, experienced business directors covering all disciplines who can be hired by clients on a project or time basis to provide input. We work with experienced professionals who can deliver results and who can also be hired by the clients on an interim or permanent basis. They are paid for what they do and the results they deliver. From this Mobile Boardroom came a number of 'Directions' leaflets giving short sharp advice on the key areas of growth to stimulate thought and assist business owners in running their companies effectively.

This book is a summary of the initial leaflets and should be seen as a series of short stories that are part of a continuous journey that EMC and its team have helped so many business owners complete. It is a guide to better business and some ideas and pointers on how not to make the mistakes that so many have made before.

The journey is often complex and arduous and the book covers some of the bigger questions and challenges those owners and senior managers will face. We consider many aspects of business life, from financial management, acquiring another company and successfully integrating it, to selling a company for the best price. EMC's Mobile Boardroom will hopefully put you on the right track so that you can watch your own company grow. With input from experienced experts in their field, each chapter gives you clear tips and advice based on proven best practice.

With over two hundred years of corporate experience between them, the EMC boardroom of over twenty specialists covers all of the disciplines necessary to run a successful company. This book is an essential read whether you currently run or are eventually hoping to manage your own company. It will be a constant support, guiding you through some of the challenges that you will inevitably face. I hope that you find the practical tips useful and that you can use these ideas to help you overcome many of these challenges.

Nik Askaroff

Chief Executive

EMC Management Consultants

Glossary of sales terms

Sales term	Meaning
Articles of Association	**Articles of Association** is a document (often used in conjunction with a memorandum of association) to define the responsibilities of company directors. This can then be used by shareholders to control their activities.
Asset Stripper	An **Asset Stripper** is where an individual or a company buys another company with the intention to sell it off as separate parts in order to make a profit (rather than as a single unit).
Balance Sheet	A **Balance Sheet** is a statement of a company's assets, liabilities and capital. This is normally determined at the end of its tax year and is often used to assess a company's true business state.
CAPEX Budgeting	A **Capital Expenditure Budget** is one which identifies how much money will be used for capital items, for example fixed assets like land, buildings and equipment.
Cash Flow	**Cash Flow** is the amount of money which comes in and goes out of a company over a period of time (normally a year). It is often used as one way to measure its ability to pay off debts and to help determine a company's value.
Client	Someone who is currently buying your *services* or who has done in the recent past.
CRM	**Customer Relations Management** is a model for how companies can manage their customers/clients. It looks to use technology to provide a database and communication system involving sales, finance, marketing, technical and customer service support.
Customer	A company or individual who is currently buying your *products* or who has done in the recent past. (For continuity, the term 'customer' will be used throughout the book.)
DCF	**Discounted Cash Flow** is another way of valuing a company (or asset). This is done to establish how attractive a potential

	investment (company purchase/sale) is. It uses discounted cash flow projections to estimate this.
Earn Out Clause	An **Earn Out Clause** is when a seller stays on after a merger or disposal and agrees to have some of the value or cash held back. It is paid only by achieving certain performance-related goals.
ERP	**Enterprise Resource Planning** is business management software used to store and manage data. It includes planning, cost and development, manufacturing, sales and marketing, inventory management, in order to run the company more effectively.
IP	**Intellectual Property** refers to a creation from an individual (or individuals) which is protected in law. It can relate to designs, symbols, images or words and includes patents, copyright and trademarks.
IRR	An **Internal Rate of Return** Is a discounted rate used for capital budgeting purposes. It is deemed 'internal' because it does not use external factors like interest rates or inflation to assess the profitability of a potential investment.
KPIs	**Key Performance Indicators** are used as part of the performance measurement process. This can apply to sales, operational and strategic goals.
NAV	**Net Asset Value** is the value of a company's assets minus its liabilities. This can be the same as the book value or equity value.
NDA	A **Non Disclosure Agreement** is a legally binding agreement which binds (at least) two parties not to disclose to any other party when sharing confidential and sensitive information or knowledge.
P & L	A **Profit and Loss statement** is a financial statement from a company stating its revenue and expenses during a given period (normally a year).
P/E	**Price Earnings Ratio** is a way of valuing a company. It is calculated from the market price per share of a company divided by the annual *earnings per share*. It is also referred to as a *price or earnings multiple*.
PE	**Private Equity** is where finance is traded for a percentage shareholding in a growth company. PE Houses raise money from private individuals and institutional investors like pension funds/insurance companies or even banks. They invest in growing companies, often for a majority stake in the company.
PR	**Public Relations** is the practice of managing a company's image, its information and how it presents itself. This is designed to create a

	positive impression to the market, public, investors etc.
ROI	**Return On Investment** is essentially a measurement of performance used to establish the efficiency of an investment. It is calculated as a percentage by looking at the return and dividing it by the cost.
SME	Small and **M**edium-sized **E**nterprise. **Small** – up to 50 employees. **Medium** – between 50 and 250 employees.
USPs	**Unique Selling Points** are areas where your company has an edge or something different to your competitors and where value can be added.
VC	**Venture Capital** relates to share and debt capital that is used to help fund 'start-up' and growth companies. It has a relatively high level of risk. A level of investment is normally given in exchange for a stake in the company.

Introduction

EMC pioneered the concept of *The Mobile Boardroom* with experts covering all the main commercial areas – strategy, finance, accounting systems, strategic IT management, sales, marketing, production, and business growth – as well as general management, non-executive directorship and chairman roles.

This book is the result of the vast experience of EMC running 5,000 projects over the past twenty-five years. It looks at what works for a company at different stages of the business cycle in the Small to Medium Enterprise-sized (SME) sector. Business strategies need to be flexible. It is based on a series of 'Directions' leaflets used by companies over the past fifteen years. Over 100,000 have been published and they offer practical advice based on personal market knowledge.

The Mobile Boardroom is aimed at entrepreneurs, business owners, board members and senior managers in a company. It is designed to get to the core issues for people who think that they want to run a business in the future or who currently run one and want to ensure it grows.

Every shareholder should consider their exit strategy and the book looks at how some best practice principles can help this to be achieved. It deals with some of the fundamental business change issues. It is designed to give practical points to consider rather than detailed and sometimes technical advice. Whether you sell a product or a service the book will appeal to you.

Many of the important factors when either buying, growing or selling a company are included in the book, for example:

- Sales and marketing

- Raising venture capital and equity investment

- Getting the best out of the people you employ

- Exit planning/selling your company

- Post-acquisition management

The Mobile Boardroom starts off with some important elements to consider when you start a business (Chapters 1 and 2). It then looks at various aspects of running it well (Chapters 3-7). From this it moves into some areas relating to many of the strategic challenges business owners, board members and managers will face when looking at how a company can grow. Finally, (in Chapters 9-11) it focuses on how to manage a management buy-out, post-acquisition management and having a business exit strategy. This can be illustrated in the form of a business cycle:

Business cycle

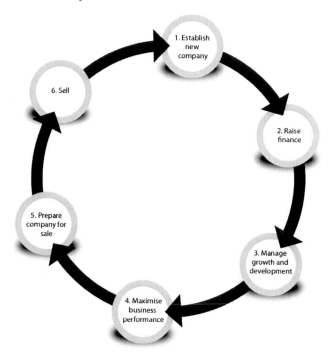

You can focus on different parts of the book when you have a certain issue you want to look at or solve. It contains tips which are simple in the way they are articulated as well as being easy to read. It looks at a summary of best practice business advice and each individual chapter can be looked at on its own merits as well as reading as part of the collective mobile boardroom story.

In summary, if you manage to implement the majority of our tips, they should help you to stay ahead of your competitors in order to maintain an edge and be profitable. This will give you a wider perspective with which to consider and measure the performance of your company. You will then have a better chance of achieving growth and eventually the successful sale of the company.

Chapter 1
Better business planning

Introduction

The business plan is a road map for operating your company and an essential way for measuring progress along the way. It is important at any stage of the business cycle, from a start-up position (in order to have a strategic direction) to raising investment (in order to expand). It is also vital preparation when looking to sell your company to outside investors (acquirers or even customers).

A business plan will differ significantly from an information memorandum used to help eventually sell your company or attract investment. But many elements will be the same. Any acquirer will also want to understand your objectives and your business plan for their own delivery.

This chapter is aimed at helping you formulate your plan. At the same time it will help you understand what investors would look for (although Chapter 2, *Raising capital,* addresses more specifically the topic of raising venture capital).

1. Brainstorming

Find time and think carefully about your business plan and how you can build it. Often this is best done in small groups. Involve your employees; sometimes the best ideas come from the most unlikely places.

Don't assume that another company won't have come up with the same or similar ideas as few are unique. Your competitors will almost certainly have access to the same market information and intelligence as you and may come to the same conclusions. You must consider the delivery mechanism and prepare a detailed action plan. This will stop you wasting time and help to ensure that ideas are thought through.

Don't rush into anything; take time to make a decision. This helps to reaffirm a plan's validity and avoid mistakes. You should still make decisions, seize opportunities and act decisively. But always consider all actions before you decide to act.

A business plan is a strategic document and should be short and simple. This way it will be understood and easier to act upon. It must be long enough to cover the relevant points of your business case but short enough to retain interest. Long and complex strategic documents not only lose people's attention but can confuse the reader and therefore lose their effect.

2. Analyse the numbers

It is your profit margins and return to the shareholders that count, so you must carefully check your figures and then test them thoroughly. This should include sales revenue projections and profit expectations over the next three to five years. However, don't let your figures dominate all aspects of your business plan. Many strategic plans focus too much on figures alone, so make sure that they represent what you realistically expect to happen.

Be honest with yourself and if the figures do not make good reading then re-visit your idea and your strategy as it may be these fundamentals that are wrong. It is better to spend time making financial information as accurate as possible than being over optimistic which could cause problems for you at a later stage.

3. What do investors look for?

If you are looking for investment, start with a simple and clear presentation of your objectives. Your business plan should entice the investor to read on, it should be concise and focus on any strategic implications. The plan should allow informed investors to evaluate your company's commercial position, any USPs (Unique Selling Points) as well as a plan for growth.

Ultimately however, it is important to recognise that investors are usually only interested in two things: value growth opportunities and, in due course, a good exit strategy! They will want to know whether there is a clear market opportunity and the management team in place to exploit this. The same principle should apply to you - the plan should help you focus on the essentials needed to make this happen.

A good plan will also help convince investors that you have the skills and experience that will support the resources in order to achieve the objectives you have outlined. These will need to be robust in order to give potential investors a full return on their investment and cover all the risks that the company may face. The plan should be a document that an investor will want to commit to in order to get your business idea to progress to the next stage.

4. Define your business concept

A business concept identifies your potential within your market and outlines existing activities and future plans. Ensure that your business goals are well defined and compatible with your personal goals. You should also give examples of your managerial ability, i.e. that you can do what you say you can.

In order to develop the steps needed to define your business concept, consider the following elements to it. These should include outlining processes like:

- Planning

- Customer feedback

- Performance review

Each of these elements should have steps laid out including the aims, strategies and actions needed, for example:

Creating a business concept

A business concept should also contain an assessment of risks and a detailed contingency plan. Investors will want to see that you have considered and know how to handle any downside risk. Be sure to illustrate how your company will build on its core skills and assets. Other information you need to consider includes:

- The size of your target sector

- Current laws that will or could affect you

- Any support available, i.e. Government grants/loans

- Details of specific training that you need or that is available

- Any USPs or Intellectual Property (IP) you have

The clearer your business concept is to define the easier it will be to understand. This will have repercussions not only with potential investors but also internally when you start to scale out your plans in the future.

5. Clarify the market opportunity

In order to plan how marketable your product or service is you must ensure that you understand the size of the opportunity. You can develop this by clearly describing your niche market, outlining your competitive advantages, possible threats to this happening and the potential for growth. Evaluate market trends and your potential to deliver your advantages and remember that independent information always lends credibility.

Look at what barriers of entry exist and what intellectual rights you possess. Think about how you would react to new competitors who might enter the market and show that there is a definable and growing market to develop your product or service.

Be careful not to give over-optimistic sales projections which might ignore internal challenges you might have in delivering your product or service. Also, be aware of other factors which might affect your ability to deliver realistic results, for example seasonal factors and the availability of skilled labour.

Think about any other external factors that might affect your performance, for example interest rates. When you have done your market research, be as objective as you can. Investors will rigorously review your projections so make sure they are realistic. It is better to exceed expectations than constantly trying to explain shortfalls.

One of the most important parts of any marketing aspect of a business plan is to correctly evaluate who your competitors are and how you are going to gain an edge over them. Demonstrate how you will add value to the market you are in and how you plan to stay ahead of the competition.

To assist you with this, do an analysis which should include competitor products and services you can compare with your own. You can create a table listing the important topics you want to analyse by competitor.

Competitor analysis

Topics	Competitor 1	Competitor 2	Competitor 3
Market share/types of customers			
Product/service range and quality/pricing policy/financial position			
Brand recognition/ advertising and marketing positioning			
Research, development and technology			
Business focus – e.g. manufacturer, wholesale, service, retail			
Commitment to customer service			
Length of time in business, number of employees and growth over past five years			

Clarifying your marketing opportunity will help you to demonstrate your brand awareness and show how you plan to satisfy your target market. It will also make you think about the need to demonstrate what customers will be willing to pay for your products or services.

6. Developing a strategy

Decide whose strategy you are preparing. If you are a business owner, shareholder or director, you must differentiate between your personal objectives and the business objectives.

When you develop a business strategy, be sure that improvement underpins all elements of your planning and include the vision and values you hold as important. When it comes to implementation, be sure to communicate your plans and ideas effectively and reinforce the messages through regular meetings. Use appropriate internal and external communication to convey the importance of good quality practices (this can be done via your website, newsletters, marketing information and emails).

An outline of a business strategy can be illustrated in the following way:

Developing a business strategy

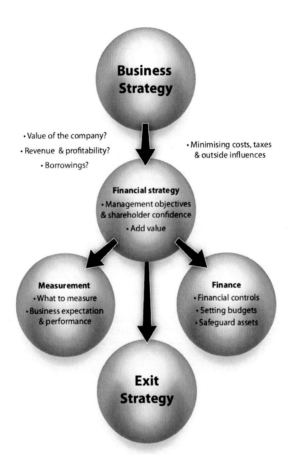

Other considerations should include communication with your own shareholders, directors, and employees. You should look at your current financial position, how to develop your plan and who to involve in implementing the strategy. Finally, think about the likely consequences of your actions and the effect they could have on your company as a whole. This will help you to plan with confidence and will make it more likely that your strategy will succeed.

7. The management team

An effective, able and experienced management team is invaluable. An investor's best practice is very likely to focus on the need for good management. Don't just list employees; describe how their individual skills may complement the team performance and achieve a group synergy.

Use simple business language and avoid public relations (PR)-type wording as this will give clarity. Experienced readers of business plans will see through any marketing clichés that you think of introducing, so avoid them. Demonstrate that your people have a depth of understanding of your market. It is important to identify your management team's financial risk and interest in the company. If they don't have any, perhaps you should review this so that an investor understands why.

Investors are not keen on investing in companies run by business owners taking over-generous remuneration packages without any real incentive to create value. Share option packages can be used but are never as convincing as seeing people investing out of their own taxed income to buy shares. Doing this shows more commitment and adds credibility.

If you need to add additional experience to your management team, don't be afraid to say so. It does not follow that today's team necessarily has the collective skills to create and manage tomorrow's growth.

Think about the operations and management component of your plan so that it is designed to describe how the business functions work. An operations plan will help to highlight the responsibilities of your management team and the tasks assigned to each internal department. A good management team is the backbone of any company, so take the time to get this right as part of your business planning.

8. Risk

As part of developing a business strategy you must be willing to accept the inherent risk in any plan. You cannot expect to eliminate all risk. A well written and thought out document will help you to minimise the risk of failure, but it cannot avoid it altogether. This should include:

- Carrying out a risk assessment

- Identifying common threats

- Looking at ways to protect your company

Once you've identified any threats, look at preparing a contingency for each one, for example if you are too dependent on one large customer. You may not be able to eliminate a particular risk but you might be able to reduce it. Also, think about how to prioritise on particular risks, for example:

1. Assess the likelihood and frequency of the risk occurring

2. Determine how the risk could be minimised (i.e. insurance) and what actions would be needed to manage the situation

3. Estimate the potential impact if the risk did occur and the costs associated with it

In order to manage risk, look at what types of risk you face as well as ones that you are not willing to take. This will help you reduce the element of surprise. Also remember, a risk is anything which can harm your company. This is why each one should be identified and prioritised. This will help each department assess and plan for any potential risks, giving an understanding of the likely impact of each one if it occurred.

9. Resources

Any business plan should look to utilise your current resources and combine them with others in order to exploit business opportunities. These could be cash, people, information, intellectual property, knowledge, technology, connections etc. Be careful, because if you assume that resources like this are in place when they aren't, you are likely to put yourself under pressure. Do your research and be clear about what you need and where it will come from.

With this in mind, it is important to think about how well you manage your resources, especially in the following two key areas:

Finance

- Make sure that your financial management is appropriate and effective to help you manage creditors, debtors, cash flow, loans, etc

- Look at the key financial parameters focused on improvement - profit, return on capital, shareholder value, etc

- Evaluate any new activities requiring investment. You can't do everything at once and investments need to be carefully planned and prioritised

Information

Consider the extent of the information you have and how it is used. Ensure that this is managed in a way that reflects your needs. Look into the benefits of introducing a Customer Relationship Management (CRM) system to help you integrate your front office (sales) and back office (support) information.

Ensure that your company information is secure. For example, back up the computers daily and in an effective manner. Check that your company information is made accessible to those who need it and define people's user rights so that you know who should and shouldn't have access to certain information.

Continually improve the data you collect and every time you fail to win an order, understand why and which competitor it has gone to. These procedures will help you to maintain high standards and manage change and achieve growth.

10. Customer satisfaction

Having a business plan which looks at how customer satisfaction can be maximised is ultimately what will help to define your success. Every company can have satisfied and dissatisfied customers but how often do you measure this or really want to measure it?

If you are an existing company who trades, a survey can help you better understand the needs of your customers and should consider:

- Identifying 'at risk' customers

- Re-engaging with lapsed or dormant customers

- Identifying training needs of customer-facing employees

- Identifying new products/services

- Interpreting the results from a survey in order to improve procedures

- How to retain a high proportion of existing customers

Most of all look at how you can be 'customer-centric'. Think about a customer over a period of time (e.g. three years rather than at one precise time). A typical example of a survey can be illustrated in the following way:

Customer satisfaction survey

How important are the following points when you purchase this type of product or service?

	5 Very important	4 Quite important	3 Average importance	2 Not very important	1 Not important
Quality of product and ease of use					
Price and value					
Relationship with your supplier					
Reaction of the supplier to an issue					
Use of product/ service					
Innovation and future development					
Overall customer experience					

Knowing what your customers think about you is a way in which to improve your products and services in order to retain and grow their business in the future.

Customer surveys may also help to ensure that the customer experience remains at a high level by getting feedback on areas, both good and bad. Ensure that you communicate with your sales and marketing department so that all those involved are aware of what it takes to keep your customers happy and loyal.

Summary

A good business plan will help you to save money and time by focusing your activities, giving you more control over your finances, marketing and daily operations. Any strategic document needs to be well prepared and easily understood, with defined objectives, a detailed action plan and agreed timeframes. This will help to motivate employees and give a company direction.

Smaller companies don't always have clear strategies and policies, often being pre-occupied with short-term issues and sometimes day-to-day survival. However, when clear objectives are established, together with a clear plan for achieving these, a company is more likely to meet its goals. That is why business improvement should underpin all elements of your planning including the company's vision and values.

Chapter 2
Raising capital

Introduction

Since 1990 the venture capital (VC)/private equity (PE) market has come of age, often described as 'titans of industry'. The main players have become part of corporate history; Kohlberg Kravis Roberts (KKR) hit the headlines with the takeover of RJR Nabisco and when Sequoia invested in Google and they turned $12.5m in to $4 billion over eight years.

These examples highlight that the returns for venture capitalists can be high. But they need to be, as not every investment is profitable. The big successes need to pay for the failures and it is a high-risk industry. This chapter looks to explain what venture capital is, how it works and what you need to do to attract it.

1. What is venture capital?

Venture capital, private equity and development capital are all names for money invested in a company by a financial backer – usually an institution. It is not bank debt. It is entirely risk money, just like the money you put in to 'start up' or when you buy the company. A comparison between the venture capital and debt options (i.e. from a bank) can be illustrated in the following way:

Venture capital	Debt
Committed until shareholder(s) 'exit' the company	Term-based or often repayable on demand
'Returns' based on company growth and success	Shared costs and repayments due whatever the results
Investors work alongside the shareholders	Lenders generally have first option on any company assets
Investors work with you through any difficulties	Lenders prioritise on either loan or asset security over and above the success of the company

Venture capital usually involves selling part ownership of the company to help it grow faster. If you are not prepared to consider taking on an outside investor to grow your company then this is not for you. Nor is it an alternative to bank debt, as by selling shares you are bringing in an investment partner who will want to see growth.

As with all things in life, there are a number of different facets to the venture capital and private equity market. In this chapter we will consider the venture capital side. Venture capital, in its simplest form, is capital (equity) invested into your company for one of three reasons:

1. Seed capital – to get you started

2. Development capital – to push you forward

3. Growth capital – to expand the company

Raising finance from this source has become a popular route, especially for smaller organisations. This should be of interest to those running smaller companies (or those wishing to start a company) who have identified the requirement to raise external investment to help fund the process.

2. Be clear why funding is required

Let's start by trying to put you off venture capital. A VC in the form of a Private Equity House will want high-growth, high-return companies, run by strong management in sectors that are or will grow faster than those around them. It will put significant performance targets on you; they will expect a Board of Directors position and depending on the investment agreement, have the option of dismissing you if you do not perform!

Don't waste your time chasing venture capital if all you want to do is maintain a lifestyle business. If you don't have ambitions for significant growth or if you need money to reduce bank exposure or fund past losses then think about if this option is what you really want.

VCs often look for high-growth companies that need significant amounts of cash. They want ones with big ambitions, who are willing to work with outsiders and who are prepared to share the spoils of a larger company when it is sold.

They usually have hundreds of business plans sent to them every year seeking investment as they are the 'next big thing'. Before even reading the plan, the investment director will look at the team behind the plan. As much as they invest in a company, they invest in the people behind it. We all know having an idea won't make you rich on its own; it is how well that idea is developed and executed.

3. Which VC to approach and how

Most VCs usually have a variety of investment criteria that they insist on in order to make an investment. Generally these will be:

- Phase of the investment – start-up, development or growth

- Size of the investment

- Being a specialist in a particular sector

A list of companies can be found online or from most countries' venture capital associations. In practice, most companies seek professional advice when approaching venture capitalists as well as experience and personal contacts. An experienced corporate finance adviser is essential to help you through the maze of different choices and the complexities of the challenges they pose.

Some of the large ones have web portals where you can send them your business plan – either by answering a few questions or submitting a full plan.

4. The business plan

Once the company is prepared and a potential investor has been identified, an attractive case needs to be presented to a VC. This will help to arouse interest and hopefully initiate a preliminary meeting. This is normally achieved by the preparation and distribution of a business plan (covered in Chapter 1, *Better business planning*).

Great care must be taken in preparing the document to achieve maximum impact.

There are plenty of guidelines on the subject of preparing a business plan but many companies seek advice and assistance in this area. Most importantly, the plan should be written by the management team and include a short, concise executive summary.

Keep the plan relatively brief by, for example, placing corporate literature etc in an appendix which can be referred to in the main body of text. Most investors want to know the following key points:

- The company's purpose

- The problem that it solves and how it solves it

- The size of the market and the competitors

- The business model – in particular, how you will take the idea to market, pricing, customer profile (including the life and value of the product/service)

- The team – and why they will be able to deliver the plan

- The financials – Profit and Loss (P&L) statements, Cash Flows, Balance Sheets

- What is being offered to a VC

Most of these will be easy to determine, although the most difficult to put together are the financials. Remember that when a VC looks at potential investments it goes for the team first and often the financials last. The reason is that they know that the right people in place with a very good idea will often produce the best results.

However, they want to see credible assumptions – for example, the cost of any future acquisition of a customer, the lifetime value and how these are delivered. They will also want a company to demonstrate a fundamental knowledge of the business side and how it operates. Many VCs will then 'remodel' the proposal to see how their investment will make a difference.

5. Be prepared to face emotive issues

The transition from a 100% owner-managed company to that of one in which a VC has even a minority stake will change the culture of an organisation. It may also raise emotive issues for an owner-manager. This can often involve admitting that as a business owner or major shareholder you will lose some control over the direction of the company. To a large extent, this is what you would expect if you look to raise capital and invite other shareholders into the company.

A question of 'letting go' of your old company can be hard for any business owner. But you need to ask yourself the following questions. Which would you rather have?

1. A 100% shareholding in a company with an annual turnover of £5 million (with total control)?

    or

2. A 30% shareholding in a company with an annual turnover of £50 million (with partial control but much more potential)?

Shareholder comparison

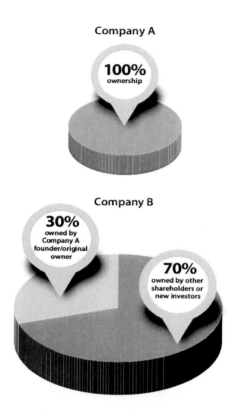

Company A

100%
ownership

Company B

30%
owned by
Company A
founder/original
owner

70%
owned by other
shareholders or
new investors

This is what your plan should show and you need to accept that a lower percentage of 'a large cake' is better than 100% of a much smaller one, i.e. a smaller percentage can often mean higher value.

Although a VC may bring valuable experience to a company, the provision of funding comes with certain rules and regulations. These are normally encapsulated in new Articles of Association for the company and a negotiated shareholders' agreement. They may cover areas such as dividend policy, capping of directors' salary levels, restriction of trading activities, borrowing facilities as well as other global financial controls. As part of the business planning process, you must be prepared to address these issues as and when they arise.

6. Prepare by 'grooming'

Before any VC will invest in a company, it will usually undertake a detailed review of the organisation from both a commercial and financial perspective. This process is called 'due diligence'. It may be performed by lawyers, accountants and consultants who usually have business experience in the relevant sector.

Of course not all companies who look for investment will be at the stage where they are ready for the potentially intrusive due diligence process. In order to facilitate this, you need to prepare yourself and your company. This will entail measures like ensuring that you have a suitable management structure in place.

There should be contracts of employment for the senior employees and all corporate and legal requirements need to be complied with. You should also have suitable accounting and financial controls in place, have a good balance sheet (i.e. don't have any non-business assets), and all taxation issues need to be clear and up to date. This is all part of the change process you will need to go through in order to attract an investor.

7. The investment process

Once a business plan has been distributed to selected VC and it has indicated a willingness to consider an investment, a number of meetings will probably be needed. At this point, further information may be requested and exchanged and a series of discussions and negotiations will take place. This allows a general familiarisation process for both parties and achieving mutual 'comfort' with your potential investor should not be underestimated in view of the possible future close relationship.

Following a successful period of negotiations, a VC will make an indicative investment offer (subject of course to due diligence, warranties etc). This will include a valuation of the company and the major terms of a proposed transaction. It will normally promote a further series of negotiations. It is preferable to identify more than one potential investor but there comes a time when they will want commitment and exclusivity. At this point you will need to decide who to proceed with.

When the broad principles of an agreement can be reached with the investor of your choice, you will be invited to sign a letter of intent which will include this period of exclusivity (usually six months).

At this stage it is usual to commit to bearing some or all of the costs of due diligence which is the next step. More negotiations may follow if any issues arise out of this process before a final valuation of the company and investment terms can be agreed. This is followed by the preparation and signing of legal agreements and warranties etc. Finally the money is transferred to you and the investor acquires a relevant proportion of the company based on the agreed valuation.

You should look to create your own investment process stages in the following way:

The investment process

Stage	Entrepreneur and Advisers/Corporate Finance	Venture Capitalist – Private Equity House
1. Formulation of the idea	• Appoint advisers • Prepare plan • Review viability and funding requirement	• No input at this stage
2. Approve Private Equity (PE) House	• Prepare target list of PE Houses • Circulate the plan	• Review business plan • Establish valuation parameters • Consider funding structure
3. Initial meetings	• Provide additional information • Prepare presentation	• Meet to discuss plan • Establish relationship • Provide outline terms
4. Due diligence	• Assist with process • Appoint lawyers and accountants	• Initiate due diligence • Liaise with advisers
5. Final negotiations and completion	• Stay calm and focused • Listen to advice • Negotiate final terms	• Prepare completion • Draw up documentation • Confirm final offer

This investment process could take anything from a few weeks to many months. For most companies, a suitable timeframe would be three to six months if all goes well. A typical period from the distribution of a business plan to achieving an investment would be more like six months. This, however, assumes that all the necessary grooming processes and preparation of a business plan have been satisfactorily completed beforehand. Taking these latter points into account, the lead-time to achieve a funding objective can be substantial and needs to be recognised at the outset.

Although difficult to assess, the longer-term considerations of achieving your preferred exit strategy should be considered and included in planning the overall timetable for a fundraising exercise. Once an agreement is reached, the hard work of making your plans a reality begins!

8. Exit

A VC's objective is to invest in companies which grow and which increase in value accordingly. Typically they will look to reinvest as the company grows and may well bring in others to invest alongside them. However, eventually they will look to sell their investment to realise a capital gain. This 'exit' may be achieved as a result of a trade sale to a competitor, a public flotation or the sale of their investment to a 'secondary' PE House who in turn may provide additional funds for further expansion.

It is important at the outset to be aware of your own aspirations in order to plan an exit strategy (both in terms of timing and valuation). You need to understand and agree in principle the VC's objectives, and proceed accordingly.

Don't make the mistake of thinking that this means that you have to exit, if you do not. It could be just a case of offering them a reasonable timeframe and method for them to exit, leaving you to continue to achieve your vision alone or with the other party. But if this is the case, make sure that both parties agree that this is possible so that you continue with the knowledge that you have the tools in place to be successful.

9. Other practical issues

There are a number of issues that you should be aware of when you are planning to raise venture capital:

- Don't always expect a non-disclosure agreement (NDA). A PE House is a professional organisation; they are unlikely to want to compete with you in your line of business. Some of the larger ones refuse to sign them. This should not necessarily scare you off but it is always advisable as part of the due diligence process to cover this off for your own protection.

- Even before signing a letter of intent, ask to see a draft shareholders' agreement and any proposed changes to the Articles of Association. Ensure you fully understand the terms of the investment, especially in the event of something going wrong.

- If there is to be an employee share option scheme, agree this in advance as this could affect the future balance of ownership and control of the company.

- Be prepared for an investment offer to be made as a combination of equity and preference shares with prescribed dividends attached. This could include loan stock repayable over a defined period and loan stock convertible to equity on exit etc. As a consequence, two offers may not always be directly comparable.

- Some investment offers may include a 'ratchet' clause which can increase an investor's shareholding if certain performance targets are not achieved.

- Ensure that you obtain appropriate legal and financial advice.

Finally, it is often worth reaching out to create relationships early on and by discussing your plans with a VC it can put you firmly in control.

Summary

Venture capital is not for everyone but for many it is the fuel that enables business owners to realise their dreams. There is risk involved as with any form of lending and it might appear intrusive to some in terms of a third party having some owner-ship of your company. There is also a question of a VC having a large amount of control and helping determine the future direc-tion of the company.

However, this sector has a very good track record having helped to create thousands of multi-millionaires. With proper advice and structure, a VC can be the best partner a growing company can ever have.

Chapter 3
Financial management

Introduction

At the very basic level, financial management can be defined as the management of the finances of an organisation in order to achieve its financial objectives. This might be self evident but it should not be considered separate from the overall company objectives. It is simply an integral part of good business management. Nor should it be the preserve of the finance department alone.

In an SME the key areas of financial management involve:

- Keeping financial records both now and in the future

- Ensuring that the right type of funding is in place relative to the current and future needs of the company

- Managing cash flow

- Safeguarding the company's assets and recording its liabilities

Within larger companies the financial management role will include stewardship of assets to ensure that they are secure. It will also involve them being used efficiently and in decisions relating to profit retention and dividends.

1. Information gathering and presenting

There is an old saying, 'If you cannot measure it, you cannot manage it.' That's the reason for having management information. By implication, if you have none you cannot be managing your company effectively. But what is management information and where does it come from? Seventy five per cent of all company insolvencies are claimed to be due to the lack of regular and accurate management information.

There is a widespread assumption within SMEs that it is all financial and that management accounts are simply a mini version of year-end statutory accounts. The main flaw in this argument is that year-end accounts tell you very little about what is really going on in the company. They are not good at giving you some interesting information. Any questions involving financial information often relate to operational activities which may not reside inside the accounts department.

The challenge is to create a reporting structure that captures key information from all relevant sources and presents it in a simple manner which anyone in the company can understand. It has to be timely, which will probably mean making assumptions, something that most book keepers and people in an accounts department don't like much. But that is better than having a delay, in which time a problem can become significantly worse.

2. The management information process

"Where's the MI?" That's short for management information and a question often asked by bankers and investors. Most small companies do not engage in producing management accounts. Often, those that do simply produce something run straight out of the company's accounts package looking just like the year-end accounts. But how many sets of year-end accounts will answer the following:

- How many units of X did we sell last week/month/quarter?
- Are we achieving our target margin on it?
- How is each sales executive/account manager doing?
- How much cash have we got?
- Which customers haven't paid on time?
- And what about that big new order?
- Do we have to buy materials and have we got sufficient credit with the suppliers?
- Will we need to pay overtime to get jobs out before the end of the month?

These questions need to be answered in order to achieve best practice financial management.

The MI process can be summarised in the following way:

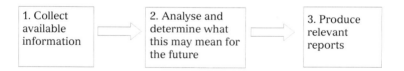

| 1. Collect available information | 2. Analyse and determine what this may mean for the future | 3. Produce relevant reports |

You need to have a process in order to manage your financial information effectively. This will give you greater visibility and help you to determine how well your finances are being managed.

3. Presenting MI information

And how is MI presented? We see management information packs that are simply a series of numbers, with no narrative. They are often presented as columns and columns of actual figures and budgets and variances. That's because accountants often assume everyone understands how to read accounts and how to identify the most important numbers.

However, there is no reason not to include graphs, or break reports down into manageable chunks so that those who need to 'drill down' can do so in their own time. An example of this can now be illustrated showing the same information numerically and graphically. The first set shows summary information which is then converted to a graph only, whereas the second set is a more detailed analysis in the same format.

a. Summary figures and graph

	Jan	Feb	Mar	Apr
Sales	113	135	127	128
Gross profit	62	77	65	64
Net profit	**18**	**22**	**17**	**6**

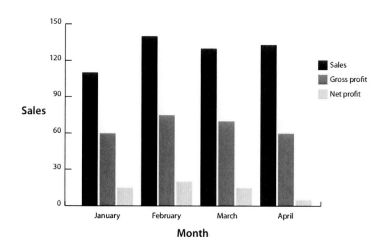

b. More detailed figures and graph

	Jan	Feb	Mar	Apr
Sales	113	135	127	128
Cost of sales	51	58	62	64
Sales overheads	18	26	24	26
Premises overheads	12	12	12	12
Admin overheads	14	17	12	20
Net profit	**18**	**22**	**17**	6

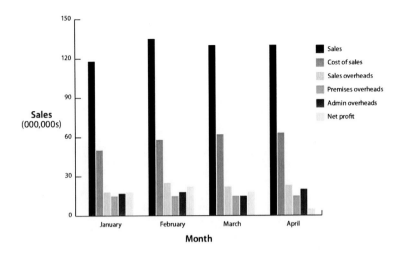

Months

The benefit of the 'drill down' becomes clearer as more information is available if needed, for example sales and administration overheads.

4. Key performance indicators (KPIs)

There are often three or four KPIs that business owners would
look at on a daily, weekly or monthly basis which would tell
them how the company is doing. For example, how many items
sold, how many hours charged out to customers, the bank
balance and the value of orders at the end of the month.

For each company they will be different, but they are an essential barometer for the overall state of the company. In the retail
sector, one KPI might be the number of customers entering the

store and the average spend per customer. Ideally it can be quickly and easily determined and should not require a lengthy explanation or be open to interpretation.

It should also be possible to identify KPIs for different departments. For the accounts department it might be the number of days to complete the month-end reconciliations, or the numbers of debtor days outstanding. For a factory it might be units processed or levels of stocks held. For a sales team it might be the number of new accounts opened.

The point about KPIs is that they act as an early warning system, triggering further action. Imagine a fast-moving retail environment where customer spending per capita is down by five per cent against the previous month or against expectation. In this situation you don't have to wait for the full management accounts to know that there will be a significant impact on cash flow, stock levels, and stock obsolescence.

It is vital that you have identified those KPIs relevant to your company and that they are part of your regular reporting that is stored with your management team.

5. Budgeting

Many corporate companies and the public sector spend a large amount of time preparing budgets, by department, by individual manager, by location and so on. Once the trading year has started it then becomes difficult to get anyone to decide anything without reference to the budget. It can be a good discipline, especially on overspending departments if everything is measured by performance against budget. This is particularly true in large corporate companies as it is one of the best ways to manage departments or subsidiary companies in remote locations.

All budgets tend to be cautiously put together. The trade off is that companies built around that discipline can miss opportunities and lose the spontaneity of the entrepreneur, although to some extent that is the point of having them. A strict budgetary process may seem like a reason to do nothing, i.e. 'It's not in the budget.' But what about in an SME where the owner can typically see all that is going on?

Best practice should mean that the annual budget is an opportunity to review the entire business model. This involves setting targets which reflect not only where the company wants to get to but also the return to shareholders. The budget process is a key management tool in a growing company. It gives discipline to implementing the strategy and is a document against which to review progress. However, care should be taken that it doesn't become a tool to stop entrepreneurial flair.

The budget projection is much more about future resource needs rather than expenditure control and care needs to be taken that they are not seen as a reason to increase costs. Of course it does give the opportunity to track actual performance against what was anticipated. For expenditure it is relatively easy; the hard part is often sales, where a huge number of factors come into play. A company needs to understand its sales drivers and analyse these. A well thought-out budget can help to provide the building blocks in enabling the company to forecast and manage growth.

On an individual level if sales activity can be allocated to individuals who are responsible for specific customers, products or market, then it must be monitored rigorously.

6. Managing costs

How well to manage costs is a very big subject but there are a few critical points to be noted. It is vital in any company to know how costs arise and how to control them. This should not be confused with paying the lowest price for a product or service.

In any company there are different types of costs:

- External - such as business rates

- Some that vary directly with sales activity, such as raw material costs or sales commission

- Others - like phone bills, travel expenses, or advertising

It is wise to remember that the profit is in the buying of services. This is as relevant now as it was one hundred years ago.

There is a very simple formula in business; sales less costs equal profits. If sales are a hundred units, costs are ninety units, and then profit is ten units. Managing to reduce costs by one unit means increasing profit to eleven units, which is a ten per cent increase. So, a small incremental increase in sales revenue or small reductions in costs can have a disproportionately positive effect on profit. Of course the converse is also true.

In managing costs it is essential to understand what drives them and to what extent they can be changed. Often the simple decision is thought to be to find a cheaper supplier. But there is a basic law, formulated by John Ruskin, the nineteenth century artist and social reformer, referred to as The Common Law of Business Balance, as follows:

"There is hardly anything in the world that someone cannot make a little worse and sell a little cheaper, and the people who consider price alone are that person's lawful prey. It's unwise to

pay too much, but it's worse to pay too little. When you pay too much, you lose a little money — that is all.

"When you pay too little, you sometimes lose everything, because the thing you bought was incapable of doing the thing it was bought to do. The common law of business balance prohibits paying a little and getting a lot — it can't be done. If you deal with the lowest bidder, it is well to add something for the risk you run, and if you do that you will have enough to pay for something better."

Before you think about moving to a lower cost supplier consider all those matters that can be the downside of cheaper cost. For example (if you sell products):

- Slower or unreliable delivery

- Higher minimum order volumes

- Poor service levels

- Longer-term commitment

- Potentially higher rejects of goods

- Having to pay cash when an order is delivered

These all equate to value! Think also about the likelihood of your supplier losing their own company if they can't make a profit! However, if you have cash and the confidence to make a longer-term commitment you can invariably reduce the cost of your product or service because you can reduce the supplier's business risks. There aren't many suppliers who wouldn't welcome reduced credit risk and greater certainly of revenues.

7. Types of external funding and costs

The activities associated with running a company break down into many constituent parts, each with a time cycle and risk profile of its own. Most companies will have a mix of fixed and variable funding needs. Companies who sell physical products and need to maintain significant plant and equipment will need a funding line that reflects the profit generation and usage of those assets over time. The obvious example is a commercial mortgage over fifteen or more years.

Contrast that with a company selling soft drinks that will have seasonal trends which require more production in the spring and early summer. It will have to buy in stocks of raw materials and packaging and then move them out to customers as soon as possible. Essentially the funding cycle is a few months in length. It will almost certainly have to pay for all raw materials, as well as labour and overheads before receiving any payment from customers.

The borrowing associated with that is short term; the traditional option being the bank overdraft that would be reviewed every year or so. In practice the best that is usually available is a line of finance specifically related to the value of the debtor book, using invoice discounting or factoring. This effectively gives immediate cash value when an invoice is raised to a customer and the balance, less charges and interest, when settled. The problem with this is that it doesn't deal with the cash costs incurred prior to sale.

Some funders will provide a facility that does make a small advance against stock purchases but it is usually no more than ten per cent of value. The balance needs to come from somewhere else, usually retained earnings or by raising equity, because bankers don't tend to like high risk.

In determining the most appropriate form of financing, a company needs to consider the duration of the cycle and match that with the appropriate funding. The extreme position is best illustrated by using an overdraft to buy a property. In practice it doesn't happen. However, overdrafts are expensive and can be withdrawn at short notice. This is hardly appropriate to the long-term usage implied by owning property.

8. Risk

Risk (to the provider of money) is a key driver. Many start-ups assume that if they apply for a loan, a bank will comply without asking for personal security. The reality is that until a sale is made, the entire company is at risk and banks don't see their role as providing risk capital. Or if they do, they want the sort of returns associated with that risk. The bank's understandable view is that if entrepreneurs want to take the profit and build capital value then they should be putting their own assets on the line.

Too many companies are under-capitalised. Whatever stage of development you are at, you need to carefully consider how you will finance the company. You should also think about the risks as well as costs of your decisions. Proper financial planning and budgeting will be essential in getting this right.

9. Effective cash flow management

In order to focus on good cash flow management, consider the following questions:

- Are you sure you can pay wages and employee taxes next month?

- What happens if, for example, pre-New Year sales are down against expectation?

- Can you pay the sales tax when it comes due?

- What happens if your largest customer delays payment by three weeks?

- If you use factoring or invoice discounting do you have any idea what funds are available for draw down?

- Can you afford to take on a big new contract if you have to pay your suppliers before you get paid?

If you can't give positive answers to those questions, do you have an action plan to deal with those challenges? Cash flow management is not just about managing crises, although it is an integral part of it, but is at the core of business management. It is also well recognised that companies growing fast out of recession often fail because they run out of cash.

The lack of detailed cash flow management in some SMEs is always surprising. Often this is because no one knows how to do it or is not comfortable using spreadsheets. Or it can be that the accounting team (and external advisers) find it safer to report information based upon past performance than helping you chart the future. This can be illustrated in the following way:

Cash flow of a growing company

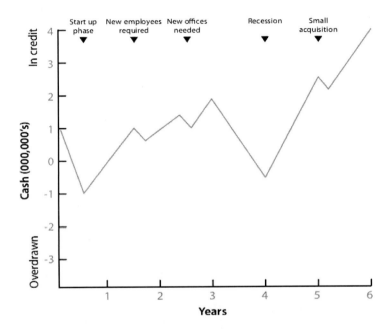

Most companies will experience 'peaks and troughs' with their cash flow over the years. Don't be afraid of this but be prepared and plan for it.

The tool that is used in many companies and is proven to work is a forecast which projects the cash flow for the next thirteen weeks. Why thirteen weeks? This is because over this period you can forecast with reasonable certainty what your debtor receipts and creditor payments will be. You will also know of any statutory tax payments whether for sales or employment taxes. In some extreme cases it needs to be run on a daily basis or be set up for six months or longer.

It stands alone from the accounting system and all it really does is project the bank statement into the future, through intelligent guesswork. You know when standing orders or direct debits go out for payment and you know when the day to pay salaries is. Other supplier payments are relatively straightforward and so the hardest part is estimating when customers will pay. That involves understanding the historic patterns and projecting them into the future. The key point is that it is a live document which you regularly update, adding a new week and dropping the last one.

If you are faced with one of the problems suggested here, you can see the pressure points and take action. That might involve a concerted effort to collect cash from customers; it could mean talking to the bank or to key creditors. Most creditors get upset when they hear nothing and then don't get paid. However, most are sympathetic to early discussions and if you can also demonstrate that you have thought it through, they will usually work with you.

Most companies spend a huge amount of money on winning new custom so it is better to have good communication and empathy with suppliers than risk having some credit lines closed to you in the future.

Summary

Successful business people are usually financially literate. They may not be trained accountants but they instinctively understand and interpret business data. Effective financial management ensures that this type of data can be used for decision making and is readily available in an easily understandable format.

The financial management process is relatively simple but many companies don't do it well which is why you need to spend time on it. By doing this you will improve your communication internally as well as with customers, suppliers and lenders which is good practice for any company.

Chapter 4
Sales and marketing

Introduction

In today's competitive selling environment, ensuring that you stay ahead of your competitors and offer real value are key drivers for any company. There is pressure to achieve results and make the best use of the time available.

Success in selling is often based upon the skills in managing a sales team, the quality within that team, as well as having the right products and services. The key to achieving this is to have a smooth sales and marketing operation. This is one which can create an increase in sales within weeks (rather than months or years) as the pace of change can be very fast. This chapter will look at how you can get the best out of your sales and marketing and some of the vital factors which will help to make it a success.

1. Recruitment and process

The key to running a successful sales operation is that all members of the team understand the context of their jobs. They must understand the market, the sales strategy for the company and where they sit in this process.

Recruiting sales people must be well-considered in terms of ensuring that new members will fit into the existing team. It is often a requirement for most of them that they will have had a previous good performance in sales and want to progress with the company. Recruiting from within can be useful, but must be treated with some caution, as the sales role requires very differ-ent personalities and skill sets from other jobs. This is also covered as part of good management practice in Chapter 6, *Management of people*.

A proactive selling role will be more target-driven and you may have rules about the amount of time someone spends on new business compared to account management. In some compan-ies this will not be an issue; for example, if you have two differ-ent types of selling role, or one focused on each type of target market. This will affect your sales targeting, reward structure and your expectation of the mix of business a sales executive is expected to deliver.

Make sure that you invest in maintaining and updating prospect and customer information. This can be captured by having a Customer Relationship Management (CRM) system, a good database and internal IT and sales processes. This may take time to produce and require discipline, but it is a sound investment.

Some sales executives don't like to update records, but having accurate information on target accounts and customers is vital. You should ensure that you set minimum standards for data-base entries (within a CRM system) so that if someone leaves the company you will have up-to-date information. Link it also to other departments, in particular marketing, so that manage-ment reports can be generated and shared. This is important to track your sales performance. Good quality information makes managing your prospects and customers easier. It will also help new recruits to adapt more quickly to a sales role.

2. Measurement

Measuring the performance of a sales team and its individual members is an important part of sales targeting and management. Sales people should be capable of working to realistic targets and deadlines. Targets should be achievable, but more importantly, agreed, with the sales executive.

Try and set financial (target-driven) and non-financial (goal-driven) **SMART** objectives which look at what is:

- Specific
- Measurable
- Achievable
- Realistic
- Time-bound

You can apply this to someone's everyday selling role and list the actions relevant to a particular target or customer account. You can use the following table to help you.

Objectives	TARGET ACCOUNT: Actions in your target account/customer
1. Specific	
2. Measureable	
3. Achievable	
4. Realistic	
5. Time-bound	

Regular one-to-one meetings with individual sales executives will assist in ensuring that the team is working in the right direction, which should be enhanced by six- monthly or annual appraisals. Regular sales meetings will help the team to work together and focus on the sales targets and actions needed to achieve them.

In order to help with this, look at how key performance indicators (KPIs) can be used for monitoring purposes, usually on a weekly or monthly basis, and for each sales executive. This can be summarised as:

1. One, three and six-month sales forecast by month with percentage probabilities.

2. Number and value of new accounts opened/existing accounts grown.

3. Number of sales visits made (new business versus existing accounts).

4. Pipeline value and number and value of accounts traded with.

5. Number of quotations/value of quotations/proposals issued (and conversion rate).

6. Actual sales value (and variance from target).

7. Actual total revenue/profit margin (and percentage against target).

8. Actual sales year to date (YTD).

Some of the factors listed here will be more important than others for certain companies, depending on the product/service being sold.

It is only by measuring the various KPIs as well as actual performance that a sales team can become effective and profitable. Another element to this is to set realistic targets as well as a 'stretch' target to help maintain a strong sales focus. Good time management is also important as it helps people to deliver realistic goals.

3. Motivation and reward

It is easy to imagine that a sales team is only motivated by financial remuneration but this isn't always the case. Some people can be motivated by:

- Recognition

- Status/job title

- The feeling that they are helping the company to meet its sales objectives

- Praise from their manager

- Job satisfaction and self-development

- Feeling part of a successful company

A good sales manager will assess the motivational needs of the team and individuals within it and use appropriate measures for each of them. It is clear, however, that financial remuneration is a key factor in motivating many people and a commission plan will be an important recruiting and management tool.

Think about the type of people you want in a sales role and the way their salary and any bonus is structured. Some companies, for example, don't pay commission if the role is more account management or customer service-focused.

However, giving a sales bonus should be based on the company's ability to pay, before being communicated to the sales team. You will need to spend time thinking of the best way to introduce a commission plan. When you do this, think about the balance between looking for revenue compared to actual profit.

Whatever scheme you decide upon, make sure that it is fair and motivates people.

A selling environment often involves pressure. Sales executives and managers may have to do a lot of travelling and spend time on their own. It involves people having to regularly achieve sales targets. This is why team spirit and motivation are so important.

In order to maintain high levels of motivation, keep the sales team informed of any new company initiatives and have regular formal as well as informal meetings. Social events and rewards, especially ones linked to exceeding sales targets, will also help to achieve high levels of motivation.

4. Training and mentoring

In order to maximise your investment in a sales executive, invest in training, development and support. Ensure that your sales executives have good questioning techniques and inter-personal skills. It is important that they know how to ask the right balance of questions between a buyer's needs and any developments that might come out of this.

Many sales people close too early without taking the time to get the necessary level of commitment from a prospect or customer. Or they get involved in discussions about pricing because they have failed to really add value. You can avoid this by employing the right people and ensuring that any sales training skills become part of someone's daily routine.

To help with this you will need to mentor them, which can be done by giving them time, experience, and knowledge of the market; all of which will enable them to fulfil their roles more effectively. This can be done by a sales manager going on visits with members of your sales team (but ensuring that they lead the meeting). This will provide valuable information on how good they are and uncover areas for potential training and development.

With new employees, send them out with an experienced sales executive a few times within the first weeks of their employ-ment and repeat this from time to time. Mentoring helps to provide individuals with guidance from someone with more experience and knowledge than themselves.

5. Marketing

Although marketing and sales are linked they are not the same. A marketing department has the role of building a brand which will be the image of the company and its products and services. It is also a source of generating leads and gathering market intelligence. Building the image of the company will make the sales tasks much easier, as a target account will often find it easier to relate to a well-established or innovative brand.

Generating leads will assist the sales team in finding new potential customers, although you need to establish how much of their own lead generation they should do. Typical ways of generating leads can be through advertising, exhibitions, mail shots, e-shots, search engine optimisation (SEO) and telemarketing. Once leads are generated and given to members of a sales team, feedback should be given. This will help to ensure that they are of the right quality and improve future marketing campaigns.

In many ways the process of lead generation to sale is like a funnel which can be illustrated in the following way:

Marketing/sales funnel

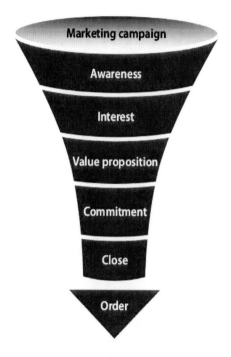

Gathering market intelligence is perhaps the most important task that a marketing function can have. It involves fully understanding the marketplace in which the company operates. Typical objectives will be to:

- Understand the size of the market
- Understand the strengths and weaknesses of the competition
- Understand the competition's pricing
- Research current or future legislation or regulations with regard to products/services

- Monitor customer satisfaction levels

- Recommend and justify the development of new products or services

Always measure the outcome of a campaign. It is important to keep the sales team aware of all promotional activity that is taking place. This will help the latter to communicate the message to target accounts and customers.

However you decide to market your company, ensure that you collect relevant information and review any campaigns that you do. Good communication between your marketing and sales department is also essential. Be informative, relevant and interesting because the better your marketing information is, the easier it will be to get your company's message across to your target audience.

6. Profit, revenue and margins

A key part of any successful sales operation is to ensure that a company sells its products and services with a reasonable and agreed gross margin. Even though most companies will also have revenue targets, without an acceptable margin an order is likely to be seen as having no or a limited benefit unless it is for the service element or for carefully considered strategic reasons.

As part of your sales strategy, there will be an assumption of the average percentage gross margin that the company will make. A key skill in selling is the ability to maintain an acceptable margin so that the focus is on value not on price! This means that each sales executive needs to sell the benefits of your products/services and company.

In order to protect your profit margins, discourage discounting as this focuses on price. If you really feel that you have to give a discount, negotiate, i.e. look for something in return. This could be a higher order amount and/or value, a longer contract or shorter payment terms. If you do have to reduce the price, then give something other than price away (and by choosing parts of your offer which have a lower value to you).

A profit margin is what makes a company survive and grow and by taking the time to build this in to your sales strategy (and any commission or bonus plan) you will help to protect it.

7. Qualification

Qualification is the process which all sales executives must use to establish how likely they are to get a piece of business, (or whether they are going to get a sale at all). In order to ensure that members of a sales team have qualified an opportunity well, build it into your sales process. This should include their ability to:

- Ensure that a budget is in place or one could be created

- Know the decision-making path of the target account

- Understand the needs of the target account

- Get genuine commitment from the people involved in the decision-making process

- Know the realistic timeframe that the target account is working towards

- Get credit approval for a target account before looking to trade with it

- Ensure that any supplier approvals are in place

Other points to factor in include a 'reality check' which looks at a sales executive's perception. This should then be compared to either past experience or known factors about the target account.

For larger sales opportunities you should set up meetings to develop the business relationship and ensure that you maximise the chance to really understand the target account's needs. This is not always an easy process but it will help you focus on meeting these needs on a number of different levels.

The process of qualification should be ongoing during the whole sales cycle, along with expanding the contacts within the target account you are selling to. Directors of your company should also strive to commit to meetings with other director-level contacts within their prospect and customer base. With customers, this is often a key differentiator and a way of maintaining customer loyalty.

8. Customer retention

The need to retain existing customers is paramount for any company. Existing customers will usually return a higher margin than new ones and it is often said that it is six times harder to get a new customer than to keep an existing one. So make sure that you look after all your existing customers, including those who may only buy from you occasionally.

Holding regular reviews with your larger customers will enable you to keep in touch with what they are thinking and by doing this you will be seen to be listening to their needs. When a new sales opportunity arises, with regular contact you will be better placed to be involved and to develop it. You will also make it

harder for the competition to build up their own business relationship and influence with your prospect or customer!

A good way to ensure you are pro-active in retaining customers
is to segment them by the amount of business they do with your
company. You can then allocate the amount of time you want
contact with them (and they with you) appropriately. A schedule
could look like this:

Annual volume of sales	Sales visit	Visit by Managing Director	Customer service call	Email communication	Newsletter
1,000+ units	Weekly	Quarterly	Weekly	Weekly	Quarterly
501 – 1,000 units	Monthly	Quarterly	Weekly	Weekly	Quarterly
250-500 units	Quarterly	Twice a year	Every two weeks	Weekly	Quarterly
50- 250 units	Twice a year	Never	Every two weeks	Weekly	Quarterly
Under 50 units	Annually	Never	Monthly	Weekly	Quarterly

By doing this, more valuable customers receive a higher level of
contact. There may be strategic reasons, however, where you
would want to visit lower value customers more often; for
instance, where the potential spend is large but currently sales
are at a low level or if they produce much higher profit
margins.

Customer surveys (as outlined in Chapter 1 – *Better business
planning*) may also help to ensure that the customer experience
remains at a high level. This can be established by getting feedback on areas that you do well and ones which can be
improved. If so, ensure that you communicate this to your sales

team and marketing department. This will help to ensure that all those involved are aware of what it takes to keep your customers happy and loyal.

9. Context-driven sales

In order to maximise selling opportunities you need to create a culture where a strong relationship is built with a target account or customer. This is all part of 'context-driven sales'. To develop a long-term and profitable business relationship, members of a sales operation must often have to understand the context of the sale and something about a target account/customer's situation, background and culture.

You should know the management structure of target accounts and customers. You should understand what targets your contacts are working towards. By taking the time to do this type of research and asking relevant questions when you meet the key players, you will improve your knowledge of that company.

Another consideration is if a target account/customer, in buying your product and services, has to comply with legislation or regulation. You will also need to look at the context in relation to whether they are likely to be speaking to any other potential suppliers. This way of approaching the sales process will make it easier to define a strategy to win/keep customers. It will also improve your chances of staying ahead of your competitors.

10. Monitoring

If you are the owner of the company and you are not from a sales background then be careful how you impose your management style. Have empathy for people in a selling role so that they have some degree of freedom while maintaining good discipline. With sales executives it can be challenging to know how much to delegate to each person. In order to create best practice, create a culture of trust, ensure that a sales team is managed well and that performance is monitored. But don't expect someone to manage themselves!

Making sure that you have appropriate sales reporting in place will enable you to see trends in sales and, furthermore, you will be able to make changes early in the process. Sales executives are normally optimistic by nature and this can lead to over-forecasting, so factor this into their pipelines (and your sales processes)! This should involve how prospects are tracked and how members of a sales team can grow sales revenue and profitability.

The monitoring process should include regular internal reviews so that the management team and other relevant departments all get a sales perspective on how an account is being managed and developed. Good account management and communication is another key part of a monitoring process working well.

Summary

By taking the time to ensure that sales and marketing work in harmony you will also increase the chances of your brand being established. This in turn will make it easier to communicate your message to your target audience in order to optimise your sales performance.

If you develop a sales and marketing strategy, it will help you plan for the future and differentiate yourself from your competitors. Any strategy will involve a combination of people and processes. How well a sales team is managed is a key part of this as well as the people involved understanding the company's business goals. This then needs to be translated into relevant actions so that the link between the strategy and delivery of the company's aims is met.

Chapter 5
Information technology

Introduction

Most companies are totally reliant on the technology that underpins a modern organisation. But systems are only as good as the people using them. It is easy to focus on the technical aspects of information technology (IT) and forget that it is a sophisticated toolset to help people do their jobs better with systems and employees needing to work together.

Building good processes around technical systems is vitally important but often gets overlooked. Technicians are generally better at working in IT than managing people, so senior managers must use their management expertise to enable IT to remain effective.

1. Business service requirements

Most people get into IT because they have an interest in technology rather than because of a strong business drive. Senior management in a company need to steer the IT agenda strongly. A small IT department can easily get caught in a 'break/fix' cycle, for example, 'My printer won't work', 'I lost the document I've been working on for hours', or 'My computer crashed for the third time today'. Consumed with day-to-day operations, it is often difficult to step back and have a strategic overview.

It is important to build a clear partnership with IT technicians and managers. IT equipment is simply a toolbox to run your company more effectively rather than using a pen and paper. An IT department exists to provide you with this service. Agree with senior management the critical IT services you require and define acceptable standards. For example, 'The email system must be available and supported by the IT department between 9.00am and 5.00pm, Monday – Friday. The maximum acceptable recovery time is two hours on a reported failure. Outside these times, email must be accessible from home and will be supported by members of the IT department.'

The IT department should produce a monthly written report that documents how well services were delivered and then review it with senior managers. This will give information about service quality decisions, for example:

- Is IT still delivering what the company needs?
- Do members of staff need computer training?
- Does the company need a third-party support contract for out-of-hours cover?
- Is it more cost effective to move email to a remotely hosted service provider?

By defining what you need from IT in business terms and insisting that it measures and reports on service delivery, a company can take informed strategic IT decisions.

2. Keep it simple, robust and reliable

Creating complex systems using the latest technology can be a challenge for technicians. Completing IT tasks thoroughly with great attention to detail, methodically following documented processes and keeping accurate records can be relatively boring by comparison. However, it is the diligent application of best practice that reduces business risk and IT downtime. A visual check around your IT server room is one simple indicator. Ask yourself the following questions:

- Is it locked?

- Is it being used for storage?

- Is there a cup of coffee on top of any of the equipment?

- Are there tangled cables that would take hours to trace in a computer emergency?

- Does it appear untidy and cluttered with no neatly labelled equipment?

If you recognise the last scenario, urgent action is required. If it does not appear to be well managed, it probably isn't! Even with systems all running, this may still be an accident waiting to happen. In this event it is the company which suffers and, in turn, its customers.

While technicians need to experiment with new technology to enhance their skills, the live IT environment is not a place for experimentation. Deploy a separate environment, segregated from the live network, where technical ideas can be tried, tested and proven. Then introduce a change management process so nothing gets loaded in the live environment without proper testing and documentation. This may feel restrictive to an IT department but will help to protect the company.

Example of tangled cables which haven't been labelled

3. Standardise on IT equipment and configuration

Standardising on routine IT equipment reduces time wasted when buying decisions are made. With many printer manufacturers and hundreds of models, each often requiring a unique toner, the choice is easier if a preferred manufacturer is decided upon. Having identified which model or range suits the requirement, selecting the same device (or its latest replacement) creates a tried and tested standard which is more likely to be quick, easy and reliable.

The benefits increase with servers and personal computers (PCs). IT staff become familiar with installing, configuring and troubleshooting a chosen product range. This heightened technical knowledge reduces problems on the servers that hold your core business data and critical applications. By building servers and documenting information to common standards, technicians can help to eliminate risk and increase the stability of the whole infrastructure.

Where PCs are not configured to a common standard, a company may have many that are all slightly different, each with unique characteristics. This can leave a small IT department being overworked, having to repair end-user issues, making strategic IT unachievable.

Most users have the same basic requirement; a standard PC build and configuration that automatically applies software and anti-virus updates in the same way. This helps to provide a common platform. With this type of scenario, IT can focus on an annual PC replacement cycle, aligned with a financial depreciation strategy. This enables the purchase of identical hardware which simplifies support and streamlines Capital Expenditure (CAPEX) Budgeting.

This helps keep IT simple, robust and reliable and delivers better service to the company. If for any reason it doesn't, discussing the IT service delivery report in a monthly IT/business review meeting will illustrate any actions which need addressing.

4. Managing IT costs and a budget

An experienced IT department should have the best understanding of delivering operational IT for the company. Therefore, it is often well placed to manage its own costs, subject to financial approval. In a typical small company, members of an IT department often report to the Finance Director. This is a sensible partnership and relieves some administration from the accounts team.

While IT employees are not accountants, with a simple budgeting and accounting system and some training some degree of self-management is quite achievable.

Most of the costs can be estimated with reasonable accuracy. They can be provided by an IT department who understand the systems they are managing, the related support contracts and licensing requirements. If this is done carefully over a couple of years, the task becomes fairly straightforward, so that a 'track record' is established. IT can then focus on cutting costs by pro-actively managing contract renewals.

Given typical contract terms, a company can easily be committed to paying twelve months' support on a decommissioned system. This can mean missing out on a better tariff where an IT department doesn't closely manage contract renewal dates and termination windows.

If an IT department doesn't have a good understanding of known costs this implies a bigger issue: maybe it doesn't have a sufficient understanding of the systems for which it is responsible? Where no reliable budget exists, or the actual spend varies wildly from the agreed budget, this implies a weak partnership between the IT and finance departments.

Giving an IT department responsibility for managing costs reinforces the idea that it is about delivering a quality, value-for-money service – not simply repairing broken computers.

5. Test data backup and disaster recovery processes

Consider what the impact would be on your company if your customer database, accounting records or your email history was destroyed! Or ask yourself how long you could carry on reasonably normally if your core systems failed? For example:

- Processing customer orders

- Managing your production

- In a warehouse environment

According to leading industry experts Symantec, the information that drives most SMEs is not adequately protected. Their *Small and Mid-sized Business Disaster Preparedness Survey* found that less than half of companies back up their data weekly or more frequently and only 23% back it up daily. Half of the companies that had implemented disaster preparedness plans acted only after experiencing an outage and/or data loss. Moreover, only 28% have ever tested their disaster recovery. A later survey still found only 45% of companies had started or completed disaster recovery plans.

Many companies develop a false sense of security and are unaware that they are relying on inadequate IT backup and recovery strategies. The following onscreen log of industry standard backup software shows an example of this and the failures every day for weeks. An important question here is whether members of the IT department shared this information with senior management!

Industry standard backup software example

			Filter	Filter – All jobs	
Job Type	Job Status	Start Time	End Time	Elapsed Time	
Backup	Failed	07/07/2014 23:00	08/07/2014 01:46	2:46:05	
Backup	Failed	06/07/2014 23:00	07/07/2014 01:47	2:47:21	
Backup	Completed with exceptions	05/07/2014 23:00	06/07/2014 01:56	2:56:35	
Backup	Cancelled	05/07/2014 10:57	05/07/2014 12:05	1:07:55	
Backup	Completed with exceptions	04/07/2014 23:00	05/07/2014 01:56	2:56:16	
Backup	Completed with exceptions	01/07/2014 23:00	02/07/2014 01:55	2:54:56	
Backup	Completed with exceptions	30/06/2014 23:00	01/07/2014 01:56	2:56:17	
Backup	Completed with exceptions	29/06/2014 23:00	30/06/2014 01:54	2:54:36	
Backup	Completed with exceptions	28/06/2014 23:00	29/06/2014 01:56	2:56:18	
Backup	Failed	28/06/2014 08:45	28/06/2014 08:46	0:01:10	
Backup	Completed with exceptions	24/06/2014 23:00	25/06/2014 01:49	2:49:14	

Define exactly what systems and data you need in order to run your company. Think about how long you can live without various elements and how much data you would need restored to carry on while a fuller recovery is undertaken. Armed with this analysis an IT department can work on an appropriate strategy.

Next, consider typical risks and plan to mitigate them. While the most common risks are fire and flood, the most common causes of IT accidents are far more mundane: user error, power failure and IT upgrades.

Taking daily backups of critical information and storing data off site should be considered the bare minimum standard. Along with data, recovery plans should also cover your vital business applications. It is simply not enough to rely on the original installation disks and the ingenuity of your IT department. If you don't insist on regular disaster recovery tests, you will never know what your IT department can achieve until you are facing a live emergency. This type of situation rarely comes at a convenient time!

6. Create a documentation library

Practical and well-written IT documentation is rare in most SMEs. Few people like creating paperwork, especially those who work in an IT department. However, quality improvement around simplicity, standardisation and resilience relies funda-mentally on members of the department finding technical solu-tions and replicating them precisely. This is impossible working from memory alone. Equally, knowledge inside an IT manager's head is useless if that person leaves or the failure happens whilst they are on holiday, for example.

Solid documentation is the best value insurance you can get. Introduce a project to create comprehensive version-controlled documentation over a period of six to twelve months. This doesn't need to be perfect at first (which takes off a lot of pres-sure). They should be practical reference documents that are used whenever IT does a maintenance task, like installing a key piece of software.

The documents should be continually updated with additional notes, screen shots and corrections. This way, high quality doc-uments emerge over time with little extra work. Using 'version control' to record the document changes will show clearly whether documents are kept up to date and used well. This approach requires a culture change for many people in an IT department but it will give the greatest return for the least cost of almost anything you can do. The following table shows an example of a summary documentation plan page.

Documentation plan page

DOCUMENTATION PLAN PAGE

	Information Services	Enterprise Architecture
SOP Network Tape Backups		Date: 20 May 2014

Version Control

Version	Changes	Author	Date
1.0	Initial version	xxx	10 May 2014
2.0	Description of tape changes and s/w version IDs	xxx	23 May 2014
2.1	Backup times added; misc amends	xxx	28 May 2014
2.2	Added new schedule details and start times	xxx	28 June 2014
2.3	Minor changes	xxx	1 July 2014

Signatures

Role	Name	Signed	Date
Author		xxxxx	
Reviewer	xxxxx	xxxxx	
Approver	Jon Green	xxxxx	

7. Build good supplier relationships

Where an in-house IT resource is limited, in terms of technical expertise or time availability, making good use of third-party suppliers can be a vital lifeline. In some cases, such as dealing with bespoke software vendors, having an account manager should be your default position. Taking the time to build a relationship with someone face-to-face is always better than remotely by telephone.

With other suppliers, having an account manager is less common so make it a key selection criterion. However, be aware of dealing with call centre agents who have no personal investment in your business success.

You may find that having one or two key suppliers for typical IT equipment and getting to know them will achieve cost savings compared to major national IT suppliers used by many IT managers. Their buyers can be closer to new technology which becomes available and should have a broad understanding of possible approaches to your business IT issues. Once you trust their advice they can save you hours of research. In an IT emergency you already have an ally helping you in any way they can. By dealing with smaller suppliers you are more likely to be a more important customer to them.

Software vendors can offer a user group, which is typical for Enterprise Resource Planning (ERP) vendors. If so, consider joining it and attend the meetings. The more involved you become with the user community, the more you will get out of your ERP system. Your understanding of the system will grow and these relationships will solve some of your own issues as you discover how other companies have found solutions. Likewise, you have more leverage with your IT supplier if you collaborate with other companies in order to get vendor issues resolved or new functionality implemented.

8. Supplement your internal IT support capacity

Supplement your IT team's capacity with selected external partners. Start with hardware support on servers and some other critical equipment. Care packs provide inexpensive engineer onsite support cover for parts and labour when purchased alongside new equipment. They also give a solid first line of defence against IT hardware failure. Consider the IT manager, without a care pack, who discovers the failed hardware in a critical server was a special made-to-order part with a three-week lead time! Using the right third party gives you the reassurance of a guaranteed service level.

For mission-critical systems consider a disaster recovery contract. This can provide for replacement equipment within a few hours along with experienced engineers to recover your systems from backup tapes, even without the need for local IT. Typically, these contracts include one or two tests per year. Contracts can also provide portable offices, desk computers and phones in your car park or even a secondary disaster recovery site.

A technical support provider can also supplement your onsite skills with more general IT support. They can remotely monitor systems, pick up undetected network problems and pro-actively advise your colleagues at a local level how to repair them. Even desktop support can be delivered remotely. A support agent can make a secure remote connection to the user's PC and resolve issues together in a real-time session. This relieves local members of an IT department, who can only be in one place at a time, to deal with the incidents that require physical intervention.

If you have already standardised your desktop PCs, the IT department will quickly transfer out the PC with a standard off-the-shelf pre-configured spare one. This gets the end-user back with the use of another one quickly. The impact on the company is mitigated, the user is more satisfied and the IT department has more time to work on matters of strategic importance.

9. Think carefully about 'The Cloud'

Cloud computing or using 'The Cloud' simply means:

1. Hosting your data and/or your software systems somewhere other than on your site.

2. Connecting to your data and applications remotely over an internet connection.

This involves typically using Internet Explorer on your PC or mobile device.

The benefits of this are easy to evaluate. Costs can be substantially lower and may be treated as expense costs rather than capital investment. The complexity of your onsite infrastructure can be reduced. Information security and data backup risks are managed by a third party.

This sounds like the easiest of decisions; however, do think carefully. Data stored outside the European Union (EU), sits beyond the EU directive on data protection. In the United States, for example, immigration officials are empowered to seize business laptops and USB flash drive storage devices on entry to the country to extract data. So, find out exactly where your data will be stored.

Every Cloud service provider will say they have robust infrastructure and IT processes to safeguard your data. But how can you know? What if they do have an IT disaster or data security lapses? Your contract should provide for the return of your data and sanitising anything on their systems when you leave the contract. But this may be difficult to enforce or validate, especially if the relationship deteriorates.

If you use The Cloud for your primary systems rather than just for backup, you may be completely compromised if these remote systems go down. This can result from various causes, from an IT disaster at the remote site to your own accounts department not paying a telecoms bill on time. It can take several days to unfreeze a telecoms account. If you have a disagreement with your Cloud service provider they have the ability to lock you out, so be aware of these pitfalls before you make a decision on this.

10. Take information security seriously

The biggest threats regarding IT security are very basic. Your employees have the greatest access to sensitive business data about customers, suppliers, credit card details and so on. Simple employee mistakes, like rushing to meet a deadline, can be expensive.

In the United Kingdom for example, during November 2007, Her Majesty's Revenue & Customs (HMRC) lost 15,000 pension records and 25 million bank account records. They did this by sending unencrypted compact discs by post! In August 2006, the Nationwide Building Society was fined one million pounds when a laptop containing unknown confidential data was lost in a domestic burglary. Although there was no evidence that data was breached, the fine was high mainly because they had weak security policies and were slow to investigate.

What damage would your company's reputation suffer if personal data leaked from your systems into the public domain? A range of visitors (including suppliers and customers) pass through most offices. Sensitive information is often left on PC screens and desks over lunchtime or in meeting rooms on flipcharts. Computer passwords are commonly seen written on post-it notes stuck to the monitor. This is why information security needs to be taken very seriously.

Many issues are easy and inexpensive to address in advance but very costly if ignored. Simple documented policies on acceptable computer usage and information security should be introduced. This should be backed up with security awareness training sessions for all employees, which will help protect against common problems.

From a technical perspective, many things can help improve security, from disabling computer access the day an employee leaves, to enforcing strong passwords. Cracking software can break weak passwords containing dictionary words, names, car number plates and commonly used patterns. This can take only seconds or a few minutes, not hours. But remember, technical measures will only be effective if human security is strengthened, all of which will help to make your company more secure.

Summary

Improving IT service delivery is about developing a strong partnership between business managers and those delivering the technology and service. It is relatively easy to improve the technical side by investing in training or improved systems, but even the best computer systems are only as good as the people using and managing them (which includes members of an IT department). Investing in technology which includes strengthening the management processes around IT will deliver greater benefits.

Improving processes is inexpensive and will enable you to get more from your existing infrastructure. This will help to create better technical solutions, which should be part of a business-focused IT strategy.

Chapter 6
Management of people

Introduction

Every company needs the right people to make it successful. Unless your employees at all levels have the necessary skills and can apply them, you will not achieve the performance you need to prosper and grow. Achieving this is more than just employing 'good people'. It is about getting a range of factors right and if you can address them, success will be more sustainable.

No doubt you will give much consideration to how to develop your products and services. The same should be applied to the people you manage in order to get the best out them and, in return, them give their best to the company.

1. Your leadership style

All business owners and managers should be actively involved in the drive for excellence, none more so than the directors of the company. Leadership is a personal thing but, irrespective of your management style, an improvement culture can be enhanced by the following actions:

- Actively support your employees to think of new ideas and initiatives. This can be more easily achieved within a 'can do' company culture.

- Take positive steps to understand and respond to the needs of your customers. Any improvement initiatives must ultimately be aimed at providing a customer benefit.
- Consider establishing joint improvement activities with customers and suppliers.
- Show your employees that quality and improvement are important to your business.

However, don't confuse leadership of people with the management of tasks!

Look at your management style when it comes to this and be balanced in your focus between the two. The following diagram shows the different types of leadership and management styles:

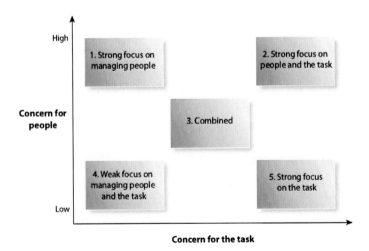

THE MOBILE BOARDROOM

Leadership and management

In relation to this, likely outcomes of the different styles are:

1. Strong leadership without strong management can lead to a lack of focus on the tasks that employees undertake.

2. A strong and balanced focus on leadership and management is more likely to produce a good team focus and be seen as democratic.

3. A mixed combination style can lead to neither focus being strong enough to produce good, consistent results.

4. Weak leadership and management will lead to stronger individual decision making as well as a lack of discipline and focus.

5. A strong focus on the task can lead to an authoritarian leadership style and lack of participation in decision making.

Good leadership is about giving people the right amount of responsibility and showing faith in their abilities.

2. Clarify roles and supply resources

Good management of people involves employees at all levels knowing what is expected of them. They need:

- Clear accountabilities

- Unambiguous, measurable objectives or tasks

- To know how their performance will be assessed

- To have clearly defined boundaries and know what authority they have

- To know what they are (and are not) responsible for

- To understand what they should do if they are concerned about anything

In order to clarify someone's role, have a job description for employees which lists their area of duties and responsibilities, for example:

Job description and responsibilities

Title	Role
Job title	Outline the main parts of the role and what it entails

Responsibilities
Briefly describe the job role and list the responsibilities in bullet point format. List also any links to other departments and expectations, i.e. key performance indicators (KPIs). 1. 2. 3.

A job description should be about two A4 pages in length. In a sales role it should have reference to any commission or bonus plan which is in place. It helps to clarify someone's role and the level of expectation and makes it easier for communication between an employer and an employee. It also gives the employee a sense of identity and direction.

By taking the time to factor this into your business planning you will save time later on in the process once you apply your plans throughout the different parts of your company.

3. Communication

Good communication with your employees is essential if you are going to work in a unified way. Let people know how they are doing and give them the opportunity to tell you how they are managing their job roles. Give them the opportunity to tell you what is on their mind. People will volunteer ideas and respond to the recognition you give them. You can also promote ideas and judge likely reactions.

Your employees often know what really goes on inside a company. Some may have become more used to being talked at rather than listened to. Make sure you talk to all of them, not just your managers. Hold regular meetings where you can brief them on company developments and future plans.

Also, think about how and what you communicate. For example:

- Build rapport with people at all levels

- Have dialogue with employees who do not see the benefit of certain decisions as you need everyone 'on board'

- Get constructive feedback from people about decisions that affect them

- Know your staff's strengths and limitations and your own!

Being a good communicator will help you to gain the respect of your employees. By taking the time to understand those who work for you, this will become easier to achieve. A lack of communication is often the main reason for unhappiness in performance reviews, so ensure that you become good at this. Good communication is also looked at in Chapter 7, *Operations, production and service*.

4. Your management style

Business owners and directors can make decisions because of their level of authority. But this alone should not be the only consideration when managing people. Think about your management style and how to adapt to different people as you will not always be right.

This can be broken down into four key categories:

Authoritative

Someone who asks (and even demands) that you do something in a particular way. He/she may command respect but will often not see things from another person's point of view. This style will often lead to quick decision making.

Technical

Any business owner who employs a large amount of technical people will often adopt a leadership style where technical communication and processes are used. This style can be effective; however, it can ignore the need for elements of good leadership and communication.

Democratic

This style is often seen as the best because it involves listening to other people's opinions. It also looks at keeping relevant employees informed of the decision making process. However, it can lead to a lack of leadership if every decision is questioned or not fully understood.

Reactive

This type of style relies on employees having a large amount of control about how they work. An example of this is where a business owner reacts to something which isn't working or wants to get involved if something has gone wrong. There is a difference between empowerment and abdication of responsibility. This way of managing people will rely on trust and competency if it is to work effectively.

These four management styles can be illustrated in the following way:

Management styles

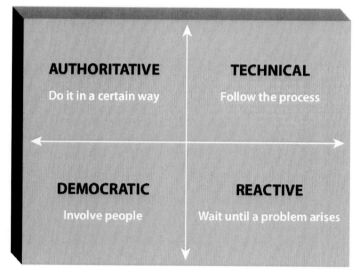

Task focused

AUTHORITATIVE
Do it in a certain way

TECHNICAL
Follow the process

DEMOCRATIC
Involve people

REACTIVE
Wait until a problem arises

People focused

An *authoritative* and *technical* management style tends to focus on the process whereas a *democratic* and *reactive* style focuses more on people. There are occasions when each of the above management styles should be used.

Most business owners are likely to prefer one particular style over another, if only because their personality influences it. However, think about how you manage people and the strengths and limitations of each one. By doing this you will improve the way you manage your own employees in order to get the best out of them as well as yourself!

5. Manage information well

Your internal systems must produce the information needed to track business performance. Good information permits you to address the outcomes for which employees are responsible for rather than just the way they do things. It also gives you a clear basis for appraisal and, if necessary, discipline.

In order to deliver best practice, ensure that your employees:

- Provide good reporting in relation to business performance
- Explain what has happened and why
- Tell you what they are doing to get back on track
- Identify areas to better performance

Adopt benchmarking processes and test these. To succeed you need to know the strengths and weakness of your competitors. You also need to decide what standards you use in order to take account of this.

A Customer Relationship Management (CRM) system and other internal systems will produce the information needed to track business performance. This allows you to address the outcomes you have planned for your company. It involves people who will be responsible implementing a business plan that will become part of your company's goals (see Chapter 1, *Better business planning*).

Good information is a key component of any successful company. Take the time to invest in this area as it will pay dividends in your company's performance.

6. Look at rewards

Although job satisfaction is perhaps the main motivational factor when managing people in a non-selling role, rewards still have a major part to play in getting good results.

With regard to this (particularly in a role where sales commission is part of an employee's package), consider what best practice to follow, for example:

- Be considered fair

- Recognise and reward performance

- Attract and look to retain quality people

- Reflect the value of the job

In order to achieve these objectives you need to know what other companies locally and in your market sector are paying and whether the skills you need are in short supply. Also, think about what level of performance you should be expecting from someone.

If a lower grade of salary will not attract the skill set that you need, think about whether the role can be outsourced, up-skilled, made more productive or even eliminated.

Rewards alone will not keep an unhappy employee in a job role for long. So ensure that you look at how motivated your employees are. Think of individual and team initiatives that reward those who meet your KPIs and business objectives.

7. Training and development

As part of good management, look at doing regular performance reviews, once every six to twelve months. This can be related to personal development and salary reviews for individuals. As part of this process look at getting a culture of good performance and employ people with a positive attitude. Encourage your employees to understand where they fit into the company and set out your expectations of them. Think about the type of training and development they need and create a budget for this. Be assertive about what standards and level of behaviour you can and can't accept.

Ever-increasing competitive pressures mean a constant reassessment of the needs in relation to managing people. This will only succeed if you and your employees have the necessary skills in place. In order to help in this area, identify any skill gaps by:

- Monitoring someone's performance

- Comparing your performance to the competition

- Investigating things that go wrong

Make sure that any training is relevant and that people understand why they are being trained and the benefits of it. It is important that they will be able to use the skills once they are developed. Also, any training and development should be cost effective and give you a clear return on the investment.

Start with induction, you may even consider a form of mentoring system using a longer-serving employee, but choose carefully. Ensure that you are clear about any business issue a training and development programme is intended to resolve, what criteria you will use to assess its effectiveness and how you will monitor it.

8. Remove barriers to success

In order to develop your employees well so that they are successful in their job roles, take action when they give you good ideas and remember:

- Their success is your success

- Encourage everybody to identify anything which might be a barrier to progress

- Respond positively to suggestions and encourage positive feedback

- If you can't deal with the issue, say so

- Don't assume you have to action everything yourself, but if you say you are going to action something, make sure that you do

The question that should be communicated to everyone is, 'What do we need to do to make our company more effective and more profitable?' Get 'buy in' to your plans to make the relationship with your employees easier to manage. If someone is under-performing, you should look at a programme of how to manage this. If you don't, it will cause damage to your sales performance and could affect other related people who work for the company.

You have the right to address employees' poor behaviour at work because someone's conduct and behaviour is relevant to how well that person performs in a job role. Look at a 'code of conduct' as another way of setting out your expectations of behaviour. Promote a 'consideration for others' policy internally as well as to look after your customers.

Removing some of the barriers which can affect your success will have a significant impact on employee performance and retention. It will also help you to co-ordinate a united work-force, all striving for the same business goals.

9. Recruit well

In order to recruit the right people, think about two key issues:

1. *Can* they do the job?

2. *Will* they do the job?

Think about the type of person who will fit the role (not the other way around!) Having good interviewing skills is another important part of this process. You can improve these skills by:

- Finding out what you need to know about a potential employee in relation to that person's ability to do the job

- Being clear in your own mind about what the job requires

- Seeking evidence that the person can do the role he/she has applied for by following up references

When recruiting new employees, especially in senior roles, find out what motivates or demotivates them. Interviewing people for a new role can be challenging as you don't know them, largely it is what they say and what is written on their CV along with following up references. A good way of assessing the competences of potential new employees can be illustrated in a simple table, giving a score of one to ten for each category you choose. The following example is an abbreviated version but illustrates the type of categorisation which you can use to create your own template.

Assessment table

Subject	Evaluation
Knowledge Industry/market Technical/qualifications etc.	1 – 10 1 – 10 1 – 10
Skills IT/computer Previous experience etc.	1 – 10 1 – 10
Attitude Shows initiative Motivation for the role etc.	1 – 10 1 – 10 1 – 10

If it is practical, consider the most important ten skills categories so that when you mark each candidate out of ten, you end up with a percentage score. Then decide what is a poor, average and good score. This will make it easier for you to look back and be objective. But give some consideration as to which categories might be more important than others.

You should think about who else might interview the candidate so that you can compare assessments. This type of system can improve your decision making and make the recruitment process easier.

10. Build a team

Any group of people need to see themselves as a team dedicated to working together for the benefit of their customers. This is very important in order to maximise performance. It is about working towards common goals and interacting with different people in a co-ordinated way.

A good team is more than a group of talented individuals; it is the whole being greater than the sum of the parts. This means:

- Having the right people in the right positions
- Ensuring that everyone understands the goals and their part in achieving them
- Recognising what they can do on their own and why working with others is crucial
- Having the confidence that the team can succeed
- Developing individual skills without competing with each other to the detriment of the overall business goals

Some people thrive on generating ideas, others on making them happen. Think about what you need and what type of ways departments need to work in harmony with each other in order to be effective. Make the best use of people's skills and know their strengths and weaknesses.

Don't forget who you can delegate certain tasks to. See this as an investment in people and think how to measure the effectiveness of this. Think about the longer-term aspects of your employees' career development and your own succession plans.

This can relate to where you want to be and where you want your company to be in the years to come.

Maintain communication with people and be sure to measure their achievements against these objectives and provide help and assistance with this.

Summary

In order for a company to grow and be successful you need employees who, by their everyday actions, will deliver the company's business goals. These could relate to sales, customer service, increased productivity and developing new products.

People are the mainstay of your company and they need clearly defined objectives, training, direction and support. By providing this you are more likely to win their support and achieve your business goals.

Most importantly, make sure that you review yourself. Many people issues are caused by poor leadership, often because of the lack of training of senior managers. If you can be objective about your own performance, you will have a better chance of being objective about those who work for you. Managing people is a big task, like winning customers or controlling costs, so it needs be on your agenda all of the time.

Chapter 7
Operations, production and service

Introduction

This chapter will be of interest primarily to those using a manufacturing process. It will help companies who, in today's competitive environment, are always under pressure to reduce costs and delivery lead times.

However, much of the advice outlined here also applies to companies who sell a service. It is intended to help ensure that they are operating a best practice policy in relation to business processes in order to improve efficiency and increase customer satisfaction.

1. Operational planning

The smooth running of a manufacturing or operations team depends on a number of factors working in a co-ordinated, organised way. Suppliers can let you down at a crucial moment, a key member of staff can be ill or, if you are a producer, machinery can go wrong.

Even if your company works harder to overcome these challenges, there can still be a price to pay (in overtime or courier costs or, worse still, an unhappy customer)! Planning alone won't always prevent these situations but it will reduce them.

There are plenty of ways in which you can prepare yourself, for example:

- Be honest with your customers and sales team - don't commit to unrealistic deadlines
- Set up rolling forecasts to allow for realistic planning and staffing needs
- Keep your suppliers informed of your plans
- Avoid last-minute changes to specifications or order sizes if at all possible
- Use the latest technology to show that you have the best information and processes

It is tempting to avoid investing the time on planning, especially in a busy and challenging work environment where deadlines are involved. However, to avoid the planning process or delaying it will be costly as time spent planning is rarely wasted.

Use a planning model

In order to ensure that you plan in a cohesive and structured way, consider the elements that are important in the process of understanding your customers' needs. The following chart illustrates this by listing the steps to analyse information and assess the timeframes and risks involved in helping you plan more effectively.

Having a planning process

Good planning involves people and process. By taking the time to plan the resources you need, you are more likely to meet the company targets that have been set and manage any potential challenges that arise from them. Developing a business strategy to achieve this is covered in more detail in Chapter 1, *Better business planning*.

2. People respond to their environment

Being well organised, whether in an office or factory environment, is a key part of managing a company well. This is because people respond to their environment and it improves quality and efficiency. Some of the benefits include:

- Processes that don't work efficiently can be clearly identified
- Wastage and poor work practices can be eradicated
- Best practice is seen to help improve efficiency
- People have more pride in their work

With these factors in mind, look at your company and ask yourself if you would be proud to let your customers see your offices or factory? If not, then do something about it. You don't have to spend a large amount of money but it does reflect the standards you set.

By getting employees to meet high but realistic standards and follow agreed processes, you are likely to get more out of them. Also, they are more likely to be productive if the environment is conducive to working as part of a team and their roles within that are clearly defined.

3. Documentation for strong foundations

Small companies are often able to grow because they are innovative, responsive and flexible. While paperwork and bureaucracy should be kept to a minimum, business owners have an enormous capacity to retain details of every aspect of the role of others.

However, that capacity is finite and that is why having good processes, structure and documentation is needed. Simple work instructions, checklists and forms not only prevent mistakes being made but also ensure that new employees do things the right way, the same way and are consistent. Don't let anybody commit too much to memory, especially key members of staff.

Put together an operations manual and outline your basic procedures which should include:

- Handling enquiries and orders

- *If you produce something* - planning and controlling production, handling faulty goods and returns, purchasing and stock control

- *If you sell a service* – planning your internal operations procedures, dealing with customer complaints and managing the level of service you can offer

A small amount of time spent early on will reap dividends later, helping you to grow and expand in a controlled way. Having good documentation and procedures (often as part of a CRM system) will also save time and make your company serve its customers well.

4. Quality assurance not quality control

The common phrase is 'right first time, every time'. This implies a need for perfection, but it's what every company should aim for. So, for best practice in relation to quality assurance:

- Design your manufacturing processes and services to minimise the chance of failure

- Carry out routine, preventative maintenance on your processes instead of being reactive to problems

- Ensure that your employees have adequate skills and are trained

- Document quality systems help to ensure a consistent approach

- Don't use a supplier with a quality problem - find another

- Design-out potential problems before putting products and services into practice

It is advisable to carry out some inspections on how your internal procedures work, but do this early on in the quality assurance process. That will ensure that you don't sell products and services which have flaws in them. This will help to minimise customer complaints. The last thing any company wants is a bad reputation or lost sales that are unnecessary if good quality assurance procedures are followed.

Best practice

In order to ensure that you develop your own best practice procedures in relation to quality, think about the type of cycle you need to have in place and how this can be achieved and maintained. This can be illustrated in the following way:

Quality assurance cycle

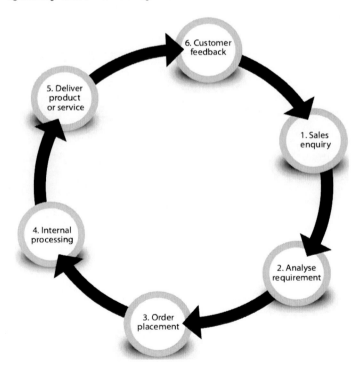

This process might look simple, but if one part of it isn't working properly it will have a knock-on effect to other parts of the cycle. This can be a big concern for any company, especially if a bad experience is communicated to other potential customers!

That is why it is a good idea to not only create some quality assurance processes but to test them. This will make it easier for you to ensure that what you sell as a product or service not only works but does so in a way that will add value to your customers.

5. Don't be too impatient with new ideas

A new idea, a new product or a new service is an opportunity to differentiate yourself from your competitors. Innovation and product development is vital to sustaining a competitive advantage. Develop your ideas but make sure your products and services come up to the expected standard of performance and reliability before you sell them to customers. Anything less than very good is likely to affect your customers' confidence in you.

Not taking the time to test new ideas could cost you time and money later on in order to correct as well as damaging your reputation. It will also make it easier for your competitors to benefit from any mistakes you make. Think about how you are going to design a new product or service from the start so that it has more chance of being successful. This will mean that you will improve your chances of maximising sales and profitability later on in the process.

6. Good communication

Good communication is usually about teamwork. Managing a team becomes a lot more effective if everyone knows what the plan is, and what the goals are. In a small or medium-sized company, priorities can change quickly, but business owners need to be consistent.

Employees will become confused if they see someone who keeps changing their mind. The more your team are aware of the constraints and demands under which you are operating, the more they can help to overcome them.

Communication also extends to customers and suppliers. Don't be unrealistic with promises and demands, and keep them in the picture. If you can gain their trust you may be surprised how accommodating they can be when you are under pressure to deliver your targets. Here are a few suggestions:

- Display schedules where everyone can see them and remove the priorities

- Hold regular meetings to discuss any issues and agree the solutions

- Make sure your employees understand the tasks they are being asked to do

Poor communication internally or with potential/existing customers, i.e. existing customers can cause sales to be lost. This is why it is important to reinforce good behaviour and make sure that you look at ways to communicate internally. By reinforcing the benefits of this you are in a better position to have:

- Customers' orders right first time

- High staff morale

- Good customer retention and satisfaction

- Good internal processes

Having good communication does take time to achieve because it requires a degree of planning and discipline. But it is the 'backbone' of any company working in harmony with its employees and its existing/future customers.

You may need some members of staff to be trained in this area so that the behaviour you want is understood and reinforced. But taking the time to develop people and the processes which are needed will help to underpin a consistent approach. This will make targets in relation to processes, sales and service easier to meet.

7. Help your suppliers to help you

Even the best planning can go wrong if you find that your own suppliers let you down. If you supply a product, you'd normally have extra stocks to fall back on but the 'just in time' system (which reduces inventory) has stopped that! Your suppliers are struggling to cope with small order quantities at short notice, so how can you help them?

Give your suppliers an order for six to twelve months to be called off at your discretion. They have the benefit of a large order and you know it will be available when you need it. You may also be able to negotiate a better price, but don't just focus on that. If you can also give them a rolling forecast for the next few weeks and months, this will help.

Although price is important when you are deciding which suppliers to use, look at the *value* you get from them! If you get an agreement from a supplier on price, get realistic expectations too. If you don't, they might let you down because of the lack of value you give to them or that they are making so little profit margin from you that you are not an important customer!

Having good supplier relationships will take time and you need to understand each other's expectations of the business relationship. You also need to cover elements of risk so that if something is late or goes wrong you have a 'Plan B'. This might be an alternative supplier or an agreement of certain targets being met by your supplier.

Take the time to compare suppliers. Small ones can often be more flexible on delivery times and price. However, they may not have the resources to deliver schedules on time if something goes wrong with their own internal processes. This is why you might want to split your orders among two smaller suppliers rather than rely on one larger supplier.

Whatever strategy you decide upon, give this area serious consideration as it will have a big impact on your own ability to deliver to your customers and will affect your future growth.

8. Pareto – Make it work for you!

The Pareto Principle is more commonly referred to as the 80/20 rule. It can be easily applied in business where the principle is that 80% of your sales will come from only 20% of your customers. For companies that make a product, 80% of your stock value will be accounted for by 20% of your stock items and 80% of your purchases will be from 20% of your suppliers.

This principle brings up two key issues for companies where large amounts of business come from only a small amount of customers:

1. Look after your biggest customers!

2. Don't be over-reliant on them!

The following illustration shows how 80% of a company's revenue can come from only 20% of its customers.

80/20 Rule example

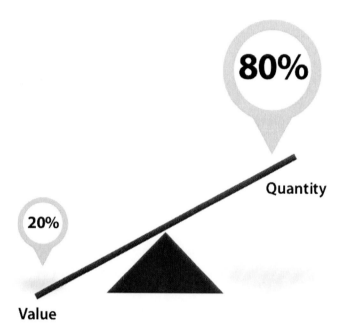

This shows the reliance on higher spending and/or value customers. It may be that smaller customers have the potential to grow their business with you. However, if they don't you are likely to find that the balance of power in the relationship becomes biased towards the large customers who spend the most money with you. If you lose one you could find it hard to replace (especially in a short time frame). But, this doesn't mean that you want to only deal with smaller companies with smaller quantity demands for your products and services.

If you have a much lower reliance on larger customers this can also have pitfalls, for example less loyalty or a potential lack of growing individual target accounts. However, if you compare the two approaches graphically, the 80/20 rule can show that a high amount of effort is more likely to give you larger results with fewer companies traded with.

The key point to think about is the percentage of business you do with your customers (and suppliers) and what type of contracts you want and can fulfil. Be aware of the potential risks of relying on large contracts and plan on how to deal with this type of business relationship.

9. Speed up throughput times

Whether you are making a product or selling a service, speeding up the time it takes to get this ready for sale will help you to improve efficiency. It will also make it easier for customers to do business with you.

For example, with products, the main benefits are about getting suppliers to deliver goods just before you need them and to reduce batch sizes which will speed up throughput times. Try a simple calculation. Divide the time it takes for a batch of goods to travel through the factory by the actual process time for one item. In a continuous process this comes to one, but for batch manufacture this will inevitably be higher depending on the batch size. This means more work in progress and tied up cash.

Reducing batch sizes will help to speed up this throughput time. Think about it. For a batch of twenty, at every stage in the process it may take up to twenty times as long as a batch of one! It may not be possible to go this far, but the so-called savings of batch manufacture may also be incurring other costs.

If you sell a service, you should still think about the amount of time you spend on internal processes and the resource this takes. Internal costs will be affected by not being control of this so think about the resources you have internally (particularly your people) and how they are distributed.

10. Resolving any underlying issues

Another element of having good operations is to identify any points which hold up the current internal processes. This will help you to ensure that you maximise your efficiency and resolve any issues that delay your customers getting what they have ordered.

This can be done by looking at the root cause of what might be holding up your delivery process, for example:

- One department taking too long to finish part of the process
- Internal staff issues, illness or lack of resource
- Poor planning
- Very high demand for your products and services
- Unrealistic expectations

It is essential to look at what might be causing a delay in getting your products to market. Have regular meetings with any departments or individuals where delays are occurring. Ensure that someone is looking out for this type of scenario in order that you are as pro-active as possible in meeting your order deadlines.

By looking at the underlying causes and taking the time to resolve any potential issues, you increase your chances of improving internal efficiency which will help you with plans for continued growth.

Summary

Having good operational procedures involves a number of key elements which need to be thought through and well managed. Whether you sell a product or a service, many of these elements are similar or the same; for example, good planning, communication and thinking about how you can make your internal process and people work in the most efficient way. By taking the time to do this, you increase your chances of managing your company in a way which makes it easier to deliver what you need to meet customers' expectations.

Chapter 8
Mergers and acquisitions

Introduction

This chapter is intended primarily for privately owned SMEs. It will be of interest to both owner/managers and management teams considering a potential management buy-out (MBO), which is covered in Chapter 9 - *Management buy-outs*, or a Management Buy-In (MBI).

There is considerable evidence to suggest that much merger and acquisition (M&A) activity does not deliver the successful outcome envisaged prior to the transaction. In simple commercial terms, an M&A transaction can only be considered successful if it delivers an increase in company value. We will explore the concept of valuation later in the chapter.

Although every company should be mindful of the pitfalls of a merger or acquisition, if it is properly managed it is the quickest way to grow a company and break into new markets. As with anything in business, in order to maximise the chance of success, a management team must plan its path before taking on an M&A transaction. We will examine areas that can help you along this path.

1. Get your strategy right

While the potential for failure is great, an M&A is still considered a good path to growth and business development. A good acquisition should help you utilise your fixed costs more effectively and get you into profit more quickly, which is why having the right strategy in place is essential. The following example illustrates the path to profit highlighting fixed and variable costs.

Profit and Loss assessment

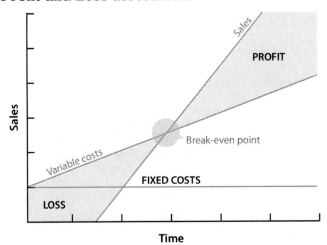

You must ensure you have a clear plan of action to achieve your vision. An easy way to start is to ask the following questions:

- What are you trying to achieve?
  - Gain market share?
  - Enter new markets?
  - Grow revenue?

- What cash and resources do you have available to fund the deal and manage the transaction?

Answering these questions is a good starting point but there must be a sound business case based on a clear strategy. For example:

'We are currently the third largest supplier of steel lintels in Europe. Growth opportunities in this part of the world are limited, but the market is fragmented. Acquiring a company in the USA, for example, will not only allow for certain economies of scale, but will give us significant growth over the next five years.'

or

'If we wish to penetrate the French market, it will take us five years from setting up to winning ten per cent of it. Acquiring the right established company will achieve that in a fraction of the time. It may cost more initially but the return will be far quicker and better.'

These are examples of trying to spread the business risk and buy market share. Whatever the strategy behind your vision, you need to be clear that the enlarged whole either exceeds or has the clear potential to exceed the sum of the parts. It also needs to give you a return on the investment otherwise there is no reason to do it.

2. Research potential targets

Having decided your strategy, the next step is to find companies that fit your requirements. Many business acquirers work as if they are buying a house. They look in estate agents' windows, then go in and ask for details. It is a rare house buyer who identifies the area they wish to live in for access to schools, public transport etc, tours the area, spots their ideal house, knocks on the door and asks if it is for sale. In the housing market, we only tend to buy something with the 'for sale' sign up. In business, most things are for sale if you ask and the best deals are rarely advertised.

So, one of the first steps you should take is to 'map the market'. This involves a high-level brainstorming session to undercover all the potential areas where you might find an attractive target. After you have done that, the next stage is to define the parameters of your search to create a long list of targets. These parameters should include the following:

- Business sector

- Approximate turnover

- Geographic location

- Number of employees

- Profitability

- Funds available to invest and therefore price consideration

You may already know the identity of your potential target(s), if it is a competitor or a supplier. If you don't, there are several professional databases that can help identify a company that fits your parameters. Prior to making any contact, it is important to find out as much as you can about it. Publicly available financial information is a good place to start gaining understanding and should be used to create a short list of preferred targets.

You should also talk to others in that market. Read trade journals and talk to your professional advisers who may have other clients in the sector and can be useful sources of intelligence.

3. First approach

Once the shortlist of targets has been established, it is time to make contact. Often, if it is a 'cold' approach, it is best to use professional advisers as this allows you to remain anonymous for the early discussions.

Your advisers, armed with your vision, should be able to ascertain whether a potential deal can be done early on. This will avoid wasting time, management effort and, most importantly, money. On the surface, the target may look to be a superb fit with yours, but in reality is it selling the same product or service and do they operate to the same culture? The due diligence process will answer these questions.

The next stage is getting a confidentiality 'Non Disclosure Agreement' (NDA) in place. This protects the nature of the discussions as they move forward as well as ensuring any information exchanged is kept confidential. The early exchanges should focus on answering high-level strategic questions. The detailed operational and structural questions can be addressed during the due diligence phase.

4. Due Diligence

Due diligence (DD) is the generic name for the pre-acquisition information gathering process. There is no set formula and the level of detail required will be determined by a number of factors including how large and complex the company is, the relative size of the transaction, the speed required to complete it and the management's view of risk.

Due diligence will cover the following areas:

1. Legal

2. Financial

3. Commercial

4. Environmental

5. Employment

However, the main focus involving a DD process is around the first three key areas of financial, commercial and legal aspects. These overlap in places and any DD plan needs to address how these will be managed and who will be responsible for completion. This can be illustrated in the following way to show other factors which are also involved in the process.

The due diligence process

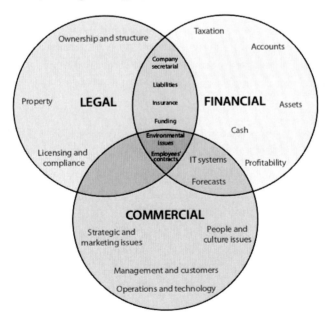

It is standard practice to have your accountants review the historic financial performance of the target company. However, provide them with a specific brief as to what is important to you otherwise you risk getting a report that takes too long and might not address the key issues. It could also turn out to be very expensive and contribute next to nothing to the decision-making process. Commercial due diligence has rapidly become the most important report in any M&A plan as it focuses on the company, the sector and the fit.

The greater your knowledge and understanding of the target company, the better your position is when it comes to the final price negotiations. So it is essential that you don't leave the DD purely to your advisers. A visit by you and your senior management with relevant sector experience can be worth a great deal more than a third party DD report. If the sector is new to you, make sure that your advisers have sector experience, as this more often than not determines the success of any transaction.

5. Negotiation and closing the deal

Good negotiation practice states that you should always aim for a 'win-win' outcome, i.e. both parties believe they have got the best deal possible. At the outset try to establish what the vendor wants and how the asking price was determined.

Often vendors expectations are unrealistic, driven by emotional and personal reasons not a commercial understanding of market value. Every person is driven by different factors and circumstances; so do not be afraid to explore ways of structuring a deal that provides the outcome both parties are looking for. The vendor may have purely financial objectives but there could be other factors involved, such as:

- Security of employees

- Protection of a brand or family name

- On-going consultancy/employment post acquisition

- Pension contributions

- The target company's own survival

A useful tactic is to pass any difficult or potentially confrontational issues to a professional adviser, with clear instructions as to the desired outcome. This avoids you being seen as difficult and you are able to take a softer position later in the process if you feel you are reaching a successful outcome. So follow some of these tips:

- Assess in advance what you want from the negotiations

- Don't be too reluctant to give way on minor points if it helps get nearer to the overall goal

- Don't expect the vendor to give warranties on matters over which it has no control

- Don't get caught up in the detail

- Make sure you see the 'bigger picture'

Whatever the driving factors behind a vendor's decision to sell are, it is important to understand them in order to negotiate the best deal possible.

6. Post-acquisition management

Once the deal is done it is time for the real work to start. You may wish to leave the company as a stand-alone one to see how it runs before changing anything. If it is geographically remote this is easier, but there may be greater long-term value in making the hard changes quickly, particularly if there are duplicated functions or tasks. It is unlikely your acquisition will be a clone of your own company and areas that commonly cause many post-acquisition/merger problems include:

- Integration of IT/accounting/management reporting systems

- Duplication of operational activities

- Pay scale imbalance

- General business culture

- Loss of key employees through uncertainty

Other hazards may include keeping the former owner on in a consultancy capacity to aid the transition. If you are planning to make substantial changes, this person may become rather defensive and have a negative influence or might not help to facilitate change.

Make sure you allow for a management time 'black hole' to cover the many hours that will be required to be dedicated to the process of integration. Seventy-five per cent of mergers and acquisitions are deemed not to deliver the purchaser's expectations and this failure is mostly put down to poor post-acquisition management (see Chapter 10, *Post-acquisition management*).

7. Run your company

Mergers and acquisitions can be exciting, but it can be a very distracting time for you and your employees. You need to have the resources in place to manage your own company, the deal itself and ensure that the post-acquisition management is a success.

Brief your professional advisers about helping to reduce potential distractions and ensure that you have a designate or team in place to continue the vital everyday running of your company. This may be difficult for others, either through lack of knowledge or fear of getting it wrong. However, this is an essential factor to get right otherwise you risk losing all that has got you into this position in the first place.

If the deal succeeds you will also have a new company to run. At this time it is rare that an existing management team keeps fully focused on running the existing company. This is because of the challenge of possible new changes you want to impose in the new acquisition, new controls and accounting systems, integrating marketing strategies and so on.

There is a strong case for taking on additional management expertise to assist with this process, even for the transitional period only. Private equity backers place much store in a team's experience in handling acquisitions (pre and post deal) and see it as a key management skill in itself.

8. Control the deal

You are the buyer and therefore it is up to you to control the pace of a deal. It is inevitable that, if you approach a company that does not have the 'for sale' sign up, they may try to find another interested party. There is nothing wrong with this, but make sure you ask for, and obtain, a period of exclusivity ('a lock-out') to investigate the company and negotiate a potential deal.

There will be times when a company comes on the market unexpectedly and broadly appears to match your criteria. If it is in administration or insolvent, restructuring it may be an opportunity to acquire the target relatively cheaply.

Remember that an insolvency practitioner's sole objective is to get as good a price for creditors as they can in the shortest time possible. They are not answerable to anyone, nor do they give warranties. It may be a cheap, quick transaction, but take great care if you decide to proceed on that basis. A distressed busi-ness may be cheaper but it may not be your best purchase!

9. Make sure you can afford it

It is likely that the vendor will name a price that can be negoti-ated downwards. The only real yardstick is the value of the new company to you, as well as the potential benefits you expect to obtain and the returns available in your existing company. The historic numbers are relatively unimportant, but will obviously influence the price asked. Bear in mind this may only be a small part of your total outlay if your plans for the company include investment and restructuring.

Valuing a company is an art in itself. There are many different ways of arriving at this ranging from:

- A multiple of past or projected future profits

- A multiple of turnover

- A multiple of cash flow

- The net assets of the company plus a premium for goodwill

Many types of market have their own specific methodology, so it is essential to be aware of current trends. Ultimately, you have to be sure that you can recover the purchase price and generate value for your company over the long term.

At same stage you will have to demonstrate your financial 'good faith' as proof of your ability, or an investor's, to complete the potential deal. You may need to put a proposal to your bankers if you do not have the funds already available. This process will help to clarify your thinking and to establish what the price range should be, i.e. what you would like to pay compared to what you are really prepared to pay.

The following diagram shows the relationship between the length of the existing contracts (as well as future business potential/contracts) and the likely profits which could come from any potential M&A.

Identifying a target company's value

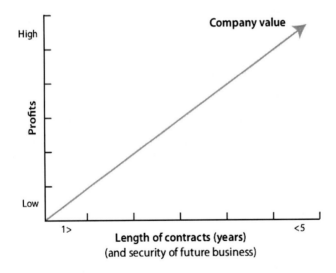

THE MOBILE BOARDROOM

The key point to remember is to ensure that you/your company can afford any M&A. The higher the profits and the more secure the revenue stream is, the higher the company value will be.

Having prepared effectively, you should have minimised the risk of something going wrong. Nevertheless you should always consider how you could extract yourself from the investment if the worst happens and the cost of doing so. This can be addressed by having a contingency plan.

10. Advisers

Professional advisers should bring experience of other transactions and a dispassionate eye to proceedings. As part of an M&A transaction, it is likely you will need:

- Accountants

- Lawyers

- Corporate finance professionals

Each of these should have had successful experience of this kind of work in the past to ensure you are getting the best advice possible.

You should always remember that you are controlling the acquisition and paying the bill. To reduce your exposure to large fees, ensure you get a quote in advance and try to agree a fixed price. It may be desirable to have a significant fee element contingent upon a deal completing, but beware when fees depend upon success as objectivity can be sacrificed.

If you ask your lawyers to negotiate points of detail, do not let them get into potential conflict with their counterparts, or exchanging lengthy emails. This is one way to create huge expense. Make sure they are well briefed by you on the key issues and do not be afraid to step in if you think the negotiations are dragging on.

Make sure you know how many employees your advisers are committing to the process and what their precise duties are. There is nothing more annoying than for bills to be loaded by costs of advisers' internal technical discussions which may have little real relevance to you. Or, you don't want to find whole team attending meetings when only one person is necessary.

Summary

Any M&A will be challenging so you must know:

- Why you are doing it

- What you expect to get from it

- Who are you going to do it with

- How you are going to manage it now and in the future

- That you have the resources to complete the transaction (without damaging your existing company)

If this is not clear, do not be afraid to 'walk away' from a potential deal. If, however, you can identify and manage these critical issues then you are well on the way to joining that exclusive 'successful acquirer' club!

Chapter 9
Management buy-outs

Introduction

Since the 1980s, management buy-outs (MBOs) have become a popular way for companies to dispose of or allow shareholders in private companies to find an exit without the perceived difficulties of a trade sale. This chapter provides a flavour of the process. MBOs tend to be complex transactions for many reasons: commercially, financially, legally and, by no means least, psychologically and emotionally. They can also allow a committed management team to acquire a controlling interest in their company for as little as a year's salary. However, prospective MBO candidates are recommended to seek in-depth advice before putting together an actual proposal.

1. The MBO journey

Even in buoyant economic times, MBOs usually take at least six months to reach completion. That can be much longer in times of lower business confidence. Throughout the entire process, it is vital that the team continues to manage the company during this busy time. This is not for the faint-hearted! But the move from a salaried managerial position to outright entrepreneur is for many senior managers a logical step forward and potentially a very rewarding one.

Although this path can look daunting it will be made more straightforward if you have the assistance of proven and experienced corporate finance advisers, lawyers and accountants. These may not be your current contacts and one of the major pitfalls is for an MBO team who start out on this process with poorly experienced advisers in place.

The following example summarises the main steps.

The complexities of achieving a successful MBO

Identify the Opportunity		

⇩ ⇩ ⇩

Experience	**Select the Buy-Out Team**	Ability
	Select the Buy-Out Team	
	Managing Director/CEO	
Finance	Operations	Marketing

⇩

Review the Opportunity with Professional Advisors (legal and financial)			
Contract and Legal Issues	Feasibility Study	Company Prospects	Cost Overview and Negotiations
	Personal/ Professional	*Price Indicators*	

⇩ ⇩

Approach the Vendor	
Vendor committed + Good personal relations = MD/CEO approach	Vendor doubtful and/or poor relations = confidential approach from advisors
If interested proceed, but NO MEANS NO!	

⇩

Realistic	**Prepare the Business Plan**	Financial Information
Strategy Guide	Sales and Marketing Plan	Exit Route

⇩ ⇩

	Approach the Investors – Financing the Deal	
Attracting potential investors and finding the right partner (s)	Different Types of Finance Available	Management's Contribution (˜10%)
	Debt vs Equity	

⇩

Forming a Buy-out Vehicle		Don't Neglect the Company
	Complete the Transaction	
Beware the of Document Maze		Due Diligence and Final Negotiations

⇩

The End is Only the Beginning – What Happens Next?

2. The benefits of the MBO

For managers

Within professional partnerships, the graduation to partner or owner has been a natural part of the business cycle, but in the commercial world this is less so. The risks are high, but then so are the returns. Other incentives include:

- A belief in the unrealised potential of the company

- The freedom of control to exercise strategy and leadership

- A concern about the possible sale of the business to a third party, or loss of jobs

For companies

- If the target company is a non-core subsidiary, an MBO offers a chance to raise cash for the parent company without the trouble of a trade sale

- If the target company is a privately run entity, then an MBO offers a more friendly exit route for shareholders than a trade sale – perhaps maintaining the name and providing continued security for employees

3. Identifying the opportunity

You first need to establish if the company is for sale and this issue is not always clear-cut. When management make the first move they must be conscious of their contractual obligations to the company. They should also maintain good personal relations with the vendor, whether the deal proceeds or not.

Whichever approach is used, it is essential to make it very early on in the process as:

- There is little point in undertaking the planning costs for a scenario that the vendor is not prepared even in principle to accept

- The vendor may allow the MBO team time to make an offer before opening the field to potential trade buyers

- Early perceptions of the asking price may be obtained

- The planning process requires a depth of information that would be difficult to compile without the assistance of the business owner

Each member of the proposed buy-out team must carefully evaluate his or her legal (as well as personal) situation before the vendor is approached. Managerial duty agreements may place some or all of the MBO team in breach or potential breach of their contractual obligations to their employer (e.g. regarding conflicts of interest, insider advantages and issues of confidentiality).

Generally this is more of an issue in larger transactions than in smaller ones. If the vendor is well disposed to the idea, he or she will be likely to assist where possible to overcome such problems, should they occur. Quite often MBOs are actually vendor-led as part of a retirement process.

Once the initial approach has been positively received, it is sensible to summarise the main aspects of the proposed deal, as 'Heads of Terms'. These are not legally binding and levels of detail vary, but matters addressed usually include:

- What precisely is to be bought/sold

- An exclusivity period during which the vendor will talk only to the MBO team

- An indication of price or a formula for valuing the company

- Confirmation of consent to talk to third parties

- Due diligence and adviser cost arrangements

Sometimes the vendor will agree to pay costs incurred by the management team.

4. Reviewing the framework

Cash flow predictability is a key driver of finance for MBOs. The company should ideally:

- Be well established and have a good trading record. It should have an established product range, a positive trading outlook and a stable market position with observable barriers to entry.

- Operate in a stable sector and should not be exposed to extreme risk or volatility.

- Have a debt capacity that will allow for greater gearing, as it will be borrowing more than it is used to, while maintaining predictable and strong cash flows.

- Not to depend solely upon one customer or supplier and have a range of products and services.

- Be able to demonstrate large intrinsic growth potential. This is arguably most important of all in the eyes of the institutional investor.

Clearly this depicts an ideal situation, but the target company must be capable of standing alone, operating more profitably and be attractive to outside investors. The managers themselves will be obliged to commit financially to the venture. They will need to be prepared to invest at the very outset as advisers will want to see evidence of commitment before they are asked to provide significant levels of advice.

The target company might agree to cover these exploratory costs initially (and the team should not hesitate to ask), but typically it is expected that each member puts up between 50% and 100% of a year's salary. However, this varies with the individual's net worth and Venture Capitalist (VC) expectations.

5. Get a team together

A leader needs to be appointed. He or she, usually the current Managing Director/CEO, should have a proven record of success, and the team needs to have strength in depth. Everyone should be aware that they are entering a far less protective corporate culture. It is extremely important to get the right team together for the long term.

Does the team currently in place have the right combination of skills and the ability to transform themselves from managers to directors? If not, take the tough decision early. Skills not readily available can be added or brought in as required.

The business plan should also be a true team effort. It should be critically reviewed by professional advisers, but they should not provide content, only advise on it. Investors will ask questions to the MBO team regarding the plan. If they have no input into the plan, it and the team will lack credibility. The team must have full ownership and belief in what they are presenting.

Management need to create a persuasive document to sell to outside investors. They are developing a strategic guide to assist them with life after the buy-out. It helps to identify the customers and competitors and clarify the market environment.

It also helps to accentuate the competitive advantages as well as any potential weaknesses.

6. Structuring the MBO

The first stage of this process is to form the 'buy-out vehicle' for an MBO which is usually a limited company (invariably referred to as NewCo). This is specifically formed or acquired for the purpose. A typical MBO involves the team becoming shareholders and additional finance is then raised from venture capital backers and/or debt providers to make the acquisition.

NewCo buys the shares of the target company (TargetCo), the trading or existing holding company. If acquiring part of a company, the vendor might be able to package that division's assets and any associated trading losses into a newly formed subsidiary. Then the subsidiary's shares can be bought by the buy-out company.

Once granted formal access to TargetCo's trading records, the MBO team (including advisers) should prepare preliminary calculations regarding its worth. In practice, the MBO team may already have daily control of those records. The maximum price you are prepared to pay will be decided by detailed projections and estimations of net present value. Your financial backer is unlikely to allow you to overpay and you can use the backer's reluctance to fund beyond a certain level as a useful negotiating tool.

There are several methods of arriving at a range of values, most frequently based on a multiple of profits or cash flow. The exact multiple will depend on the strength of the company. It will involve issues such as growth potential, cash generation, profit margins and turnover.

It is necessary to be clear about the future profit stream. The audited accounts may be no guide to the real profit under new ownership. The current owners will often argue that the 'real' profit is much higher than reported because of their lifestyle being funded by the company. As a purchaser, do not be seduced by these arguments. What could the company have done if it had not been starved of working capital or the owner had greater ambition? Keep the money back for future investment rather than paying someone twice for their lifestyle business.

The investor will carefully read your business plan, but before committing irrevocably to anything will undertake due diligence (as outlined in Chapter 8, *Mergers and acquisitions*). This is the equivalent of the house purchaser's full structural survey. Everything from the firm's trading background to its financial reporting system will be subject to close scrutiny throughout the process by third party advisers. Some backers will insist on psychometric profiling of the management team.

The MBO team may be familiar with all these issues when buying from the founder but this will not always be the case. That is why in these instances, the due diligence exercise can be as important for the team as for the investors.

7. Financing the MBO

Finance comes from three main areas and the mix is dependent on the company's financial situation, industry characteristics, desired risk levels and VC requirements. This will be:

1. Senior debt – secured bank lending

2. Mezzanine debt – higher-cost debt with less good security

3. Equity – the risk capital supplied by the team, the existing owners and/or its VC backers

It is important that everyone involved recognises the basic principles behind each debt and equity option available. Typically the more debt that can be raised, the greater percentage of equity that can be retained by the MBO team, but it is important not to layer in too much debt, and create too heavy a repayment burden.

Senior debt

This common form of debt refers to secured lending by banks and is the least expensive form of finance available. It can comprise of an overdraft (usually for working capital) and a term loan - which is characterised by regular repayments over a fixed period. Senior debt is relatively cheap because it has priority in terms of interest and principal payments and is secured upon the company's assets.

The lending bank is also likely to require clauses that oblige the borrower to maintain certain financial performance ratios. The provider of senior debt will of course require security. This will usually be in the form of the assets of the TargetCo, such as property or debtors.

Mezzanine debt

This is a form of 'stretched senior debt' or intermediate capital. It is commonly used when it is not possible to bank the deal entirely with standard senior finance. It is often secured by way of a second charge on assets and as it is second tier debt it ranks behind senior debt when it comes to repayment. This is why it carries more risk for the lender, increasing its expense for the borrower.

Equity

The majority of buy-out equity funding will typically emerge from three sources:

- The MBO team

- Institutional investors

- The seller(s)

The management team will usually put up a relatively small proportion of the total equity – though clearly the more they supply, the greater will be the benefit in terms of control and increased company value. If the team wishes to attract outside investment, they must demonstrate some personal commitment to the deal and share some of the financial risk.

The actual investment required from managers is rarely over one year's salary. Nevertheless, they should take care not to overextend themselves. Investors want managers to be committed to the success of the buy-out without feeling too much pressure from this.

While it is rare for a VC to involve themselves with the day-to-day running of the company, this is a crucial relationship. That is why careful selection should be made when considering potential investors.

The return required by the investor will vary according to market conditions but VCs typically require an Internal Rate of Return (IRR) of approximately thirty. They then try to outperform other means of investment possibilities, trading considerable risk and effort for potentially high returns. A 30% IRR is the compound rate of growth in an investment that increases the total value by four to five times in as many years. The VC places pressure on the MBO team to deliver results, but this also means that you will receive considerable assistance if necessary. They have a large interest in ensuring your success.

8. The exit of the institutional investor/sale of the company

The VC typically aims to realise a capital gain within three to five years. This is achieved from a carefully planned exit route and management should plan for this from the outset. Possibilities to consider include the sale of the company to a trade buyer and a flotation of NewCo, raising profile and capital capacity, but with constraints. It could also include the MBO team (possibly with another venture capitalist) buying out the institutional investor.

For an attractive exit, the company should:

- Have satisfactorily improved sales and profits consistently over the last two to three years
- Be capable of reasonable growth over the medium term
- Have a management team who remain committed to the development of the company
- Have increased its customer base, maintained a healthy cash flow and have repaid most or all of its debt through trading profits

The MBO team should not expect to exit at the same time as the VC, as this would jeopardise the short-term future of the company (and therefore its value to potential investors at this stage).

However, particularly with trade sales, there may be a phased exit of the management team as well.

It is increasingly common for the seller to assist with the funding of the transaction by deferring part of the consideration for a fixed period after completion (Vendor Assisted Sale). This is particularly the case where the seller has initiated the MBO discussions and banks are very comfortable with this arrangement. They take the view that the transition from seller to MBO team will be smoother where the seller has a continuing vested interest. This can be illustrated in the following way:

MBO finance example

Below is a possible structure which demonstrates the management buy-out of **TargetCo** by its management team (via **NewCo**)

Financial Sources	Millions	Funding Requirements	Millions
Ordinary Equity		Price (paid to vendor)	3.00
'A' Shares (MBO team)	0.30		
'B' Shares (venture capitalist)	0.20	Working Capital	0.50
Preference Shares		Fees/Costs (re. Arranging MBO)	0.10
Venture Capitalist	1.10		
Bank Debt			
Mezzanine Finance	0.50		
Senior Debt (Term Loan)	1.00		
Senior Debt (Overdraft)	0.50		
TOTAL SOURCES	3.60	Total Requirements	3.60

Shareholding structure: MBO team holds 60% of the equity; VC holds 40%. This is in spite of the MBO team only providing 10% of the funding (a common benchmark).

Then, driven by a strong, incentivised management team, with support from the venture capitalist, the company does well. At the end of 5 years, **NewCo**, now a profitable entity with strong cash flow has repaid its loans with trading profits and is sold to a trade buyer for 1.5 times the original price.

Sale price	4.5m
Costs/fees	-0.1m
Redemption of preference shares (prefs)	-1.1m
Total Received by Equity Shareholders	**3.3m**

Management receive 60% of 3.3m = 1.98m = *6.6 times original investment*

VC receives 40% of 3.3m = 1.32m, plus redeemable preferences of 1.1m = 2.42m

= 1.86 times the original investment.

Source: 3i Group

A business owner's exit strategy is covered in Chapter 11, *Selling your company*.

9. Proceeding with an MBO

Make sure that you have the company in a good position when you proceed with an MBO. Timing is vital and the company should be on an upward curve with growth potential. Be clear as to your management team. You need the right people in the right positions for it to manage and grow (not only your previous colleagues who were your ...friends!) Make sure the team understand the deal and what they will be putting in and getting out if it is successful.

You should pick your advisers with care and they should line up a number of VCs for you to see. Remember, this is a 'two-way street' with you interviewing them for compatibility as much as they are interviewing you.

The business plan is critical. It should be a precise document that sells the opportunity as well as detailing the way that you are going to run and grow the company (see Chapter 1, *Better business planning*).

Once you have lined up your VCs, make sure that you negotiate strongly. You may only get one chance to finally maximise on your investment. That is why every share you give away should only be where it adds significant value whether to the team or an investor!

Summary

Any ambitious business person would love the chance to run their own company. Being part of an MBO team may be the best opportunity you get to do this. If correctly managed and delivered, this can be the path to significant wealth and the most exciting and rewarding journey you ever take. That is why you need to put in the necessary investment of time and get the right team behind you.

Chapter 10
Post-acquisition management

Introduction

Acquisitions should be one of the options that every growing company considers, whatever its size. At some point in the business lifecycle, the opportunity to acquire or merge with another company may arise. But most managers, even in larger corporate entities, have little if any experience in dealing with an acquisition.

Contrary to what some might say, the most straight-forward part of acquiring a company is actually buying it. With lawyers managing the contracts, accountants doing due diligence, and corporate finance teams structuring the funding, it is relatively easy to call for help to complete a transaction.

But when this is done and the advisers move on to their next transaction, you find yourself alone, as a board, to get on with the real work of integration. This is both for your original company and that of the acquisition target into the newly enlarged group. Unfortunately, the often stated statistic is that 75% of deals are successful for vendors but only 25% for buyers and this is mainly due to poor post-acquisition management.

The aim of this chapter is to give a few key ideas of how to suc-cessfully manage the post-acquisition process. It is designed to help you fulfil the objectives that led you to want to acquire a company in the first place.

1. Set clear integration objectives

The process of successful post-acquisition management begins before the deal is done. Don't look to complete a transaction without planning the integration process. Any well thought-out acquisition strategy should already have identified how the target company will help the purchaser achieve its strategic aims. It should also use intelligence gathered during the due diligence process to form the basis for a post- acquisition management plan. It is essential that this plan is well advanced, if not finalised and agreed, before completion of the potential purchase.

By clearly detailing why you are undertaking an acquisition and setting these reasons out, clear integration objectives can be created. For example:

Reasons (for acquisition)	Integration objective
To buy market share	Maintain the customer base of the target
To reduce duplicated cost in an enlarged business	Reduce headcount and property costs by putting companies onto one site
To purchase important technology	Integrate technology into current company

Having identified your *integration objectives*, you are then in a position to plan the process. Don't forget that for many smaller companies this will probably include a plan for the purchasing company as well as that of the newly acquired one.

2. Appoint an integration team

Whatever happens after the acquisition, appoint an integration team and identify an integration manager to take responsibility after the transaction has taken place. This could mean a dedicated resource to manage a detailed integration. This is particularly the case if rapid synergies and economies of scale are planned as part of the acquisition strategy.

Whichever route you choose, being able to present and implement a professional, logical and well thought-out plan is the first step towards a successful integration process. An integration manager may require a team to help the process (especially where rapid change needs to be managed). Typically this should consist of managers from both companies.

Some of the keys to achieving successful integration include meeting regularly and managing the integration process on a day-to-day level. It is also important to provide necessary feedback to both organisations. The constitution of this team is vital and the practical resource available to it should be given careful consideration as short-term costs may enable long-term gains.

3. Document the post-acquisition plan

The post-acquisition plan should be detailed and comprehensive, identifying all of the critical action points (especially where rapid change is envisaged). It may be developed into a Gantt chart listing numerous tasks, the order in which they need to be completed and any critical paths along the way. Practically, one of the first jobs is to assign responsibilities and ensure the essentials are completed within agreed and necessary time scales.

However, everything will not happen on its own. Like any plan it must be capable of being revised as the acquiring company learns more about the company it has acquired. Changes should be strictly controlled and their effects need to be fully understood and the documentation process will help with this.

4. Communicate the plan

Whether you decide to let the acquired company continue to trade with no interference for a period of time or make changes, a clear communication plan should be defined. This is possibly the most important part of any acquisition and could include a formal marketing campaign to *sell* the benefits of the acquiring and acquired companies coming under the same ownership.

It is often easy for the relatively few people involved in the pre-acquisition, due diligence and negotiation process to forget that they are in the minority from the new combined company. The vast majority of people whose lives may be affected by the transaction will have very little information about the future company's plans. This may involve those who will be in charge and who will help determine what changes may be required.

Planning a strategy to tackle the communication issues should include consideration of employees in the acquired and acquiring companies as well as customers, suppliers (and any sub-contractors). In certain instances, communication with providers of finance and even the local community may be a relevant consideration.

Do not leave things to rumour. With modern communication tools it is relatively easy to present to people quickly, clearly and concisely. There is no need to detail all the challenges to each group. But you can make sure that what you do say leaves them with a clear understanding of how the acquisition impacts on them, for example:

- What to say on both company's websites

- New bank details for customers (if the acquired company moves its bank account to the acquirer's)

- Trade insurance details for suppliers

- Integration plans with the acquired organisation's employees

Most importantly, have a well-planned campaign to ensure that your target accounts and existing customers know what is happening and the benefits to them.

5. Keep employees informed

Do not underestimate the potential detrimental effect of poor staff morale on the new company as part of the change process. Even if all the issues cannot be addressed immediately, it is better to communicate them and the potential solutions clearly and concisely. This includes updating people as decisions are made, rather than to say nothing and leave employees in an 'information void'. Consider the following actions when devising your employee communication strategy:

- Have briefing meetings for the senior employees of the acquired company.

- Drive an initial briefing meeting down through the company hierarchy, possibly with the help of pre-prepared presentation material to ensure a consistent message.

- Devise a feedback mechanism for questions to be raised and answered. This can be done through a regular internal newsletter which can be prepared for the duration of the integration process.

- Introduce workshop programs to bring the people from the two companies together. This is not only to assist with the integration process, but also to exchange best practices and identify as well as share good ideas.

An important element of a successful integration is to define what success looks like after the acquisition. This can be illustrated in the following way by looking at how elements like having a vision, can contribute to its success in the future.

Define business success

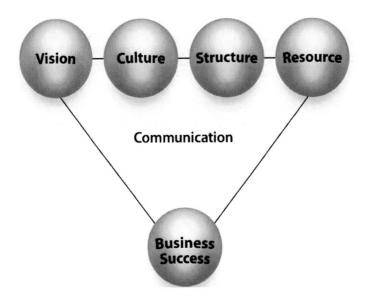

Finally, take great care considering all human resource (HR) management issues, especially where employee contracts, benefits or working practices may have to be amended. If managed carefully you can normally make most of the changes you want. This is important so as to avoid any conflict which could lead to potential litigation between employer and employee!

6. Implementing key financial controls

Take care not to become obsessed with changing the financial reporting formats of the acquired company. This might be at the expense of understanding and maintaining more funda-mental matters during the integration process. The following actions are among those which need to be considered:

- Completion accounts may have to be finalised quickly to prove the net asset base acquired and possibly to confirm any initial payment after completion.

- Review authorisation levels (including recruitment, purchas-ing, capital expenditure) and bank mandates etc to ensure they are appropriate on an ongoing basis. This is especially relevant if personnel have changed or weaknesses were identified during the due diligence process.

- Ensure a comprehensive cash management system is in place. It is easy to monitor cash from 'day one', even if it takes a little longer to get to grips with the accounts.

- Consider setting up a sensible treasury management system for the enlarged operation.

- Make sure you understand and endorse pricing/costing systems and that they are consistent with your understanding of the 'cost structure' of the company.

- Agree a budget as soon as is practically possible with the acquired operation. This process should include the identification of a number of Key Performance Indicators (KPIs), which will probably not all be financial. This way they can be monitored independently of the accounts. Take care to manage this process with the acquired company as they may not see your 'acquisition projections' as realistic. This can highlight potentially difficult actions which might need to be implemented.

- Agree a reasonable timetable and format for management accounts and their review. This needs to reflect the quality of employees available and past performance. It should also look at the pressures that due diligence, completion accounts and post-completion information requests put on the management team. You should allow time for sufficient planning to enable revenue targets to be set in order to monitor future performance.

All of the above points should be concluded quickly, leaving time to review the information from both companies. This helps to establish which has the best areas of reporting.

A summary of the key financial ratios should include:

- **Solvency** - Measures the soundness of the company and the control of cash

- **Efficiency** - Measures how efficiently a company uses and controls its assets

- **Profitability** - Measures how well the company performs

Once the main controls are identified and prioritised, set about planning how to integrate the finance functions of the organisations. If this does not come under one function, at least make provision for the same platforms, procedures and reporting timetables.

7. Maintaining the customer base

It is essential that any potential damage to the customer base needs to be minimised. Due diligence should flag up any contractual relationships which can be terminated on change of ownership. These matters need to be quickly addressed with the assistance of legal advice if necessary. Organising briefings for major customers to explain the impact of any changes should be considered a priority. This is especially relevant if rumours of the acquisition have been prevalent in the marketplace.

Consider preparing standard letters for those smaller customers it is not possible to deal with personally. Above all, ensure that operational procedures within the company do not suffer over the critical first few months of an acquisition. This way it will help to ensure that quality and continuity of customer service remain unaffected. Some kind of customer survey program could be effective over this period and may also provide additional external 'intelligence' for the acquiring operation.

8. Identify supplier savings

Purchasing is integral to the supply chain. An acquisition provides an opportunity for both operations to compare cost prices of similar products and terms and conditions across suppliers.

If either company achieves favourable terms with the same suppliers or specific bought-in products and services, the opportunity for a 'quick gain' is evident. But long-term relations and reliability need to be considered. It may also be an appropriate time to consider a rationalisation of the supplier base for both companies.

The product and supply chain relationship is often looked at by deciding what to *Keep, Create, Reduce and Eliminate*. This can be illustrated in the following way:

Product/supply chain

KEEP	CREATE
Products/services to retain and grow	New products/services to be introduced
REDUCE	**ELIMINATE**
Any products/services to be discontinued or removed over time	Suppliers/products not required or to be immediately replaced

Do not overlook the potential benefits a larger acquiring company with an established purchasing operation can potentially provide to a smaller acquired company. For example, the latter may not have the resources of a specialist buying function or modern processes and systems.

9. Focus on essential administration and IT

While it is desirable to achieve best practice and common IT systems as quickly as possible, don't underestimate the time and resource required to install and test this (see Chapter 5, *Information technology*). Unless there are critical reasons to implement change quickly, undergo an IT and systems review after a reasonable period following completion of the acquisition. The same can be said for internal administration systems. It is best to concentrate on resolving issues which will affect the new company's ability to trade effectively. For example:

- Legal issues (including statutory matters)

- Changes to banking facilities

- Reviews of adequacy of insurances, leases and customer contracts etc

To ensure best practice, these should all be done before a longer-term review of internal procedures and standard forms takes place.

10. Understand the commercial risks

Making an acquisition can be a risky business. Having a mechanism to control risk is highly advisable. Part of the pre-acquisition planning (and early post-completion activity) should involve a review of 'mission critical' factors. It should also include a previously agreed action plan in the unfortunate circumstance that something goes wrong.

Critical factors could include:

- The identification of key people and what to do if they leave

- Important customers/contracts and what to do if they become vulnerable

- Financial performance below agreed revenue targets

- The responsibility for any required corrective action

Risk management should be on any company's agenda and needs to take a high profile. It should a have a very clear framework set out in order to address any new issues which can arise as part of the post-acquisition process.

Summary

A successful acquisition must include good and detailed planning. Responsibility for the integration process should be clearly identified to the person responsible for implementing the relevant tasks. The importance of clearly communicating the plan and the process of its implementation to all employees involved must not be underestimated.

Acquisitions are a proven part of growth and, if managed correctly, they can significantly boost a company's critical mass, profile and profitability. You must plan effectively and allocate resources not only to the transaction but also to the post-acquisition management process. The signing of the completion papers is only the start of ensuring that the acquisition integration strategy is a success.

Chapter 11
Selling your company

Introduction

Sooner or later every company is either sold, merges, ceases trading or becomes insolvent! Hopefully, after years of hard work, yours will fall into the first category. This is likely to be the most important transaction that you will ever make so it is vital to get it right.

Some business owners have an exit plan when they start a company. However, most rarely think about it until an offer arrives or they decide that it is time to 'cash in' the rewards of their labours. This chapter will focus on the steps you (and any shareholders) should take if you decide to sell the company.

1. Get your strategy right

If you are the majority shareholder of a company and you are considering selling it examine the reasons why. For example:

- Are you tired of the day-to-day pressure of running it?
- Do you see your profitability at its peak?
- Have you received an offer?
- Do you feel that you've taken it as far as you can?
- Do you want to retire and enjoy life more?

You may feel that your company will need to access new technology or new markets, or it has grown to a size where you are unwilling or unable to manage it. In these cases the buyer is likely to be someone with the financial and managerial capability to take it forward. This is more likely to be a company of a larger size.

Whatever the reason, you need to be clear in your own mind about why you are selling. This will involve planning an exit strategy and executing it in the right way. You will certainly be asked about your reasons for wanting to sell early in the process so have the answers prepared. It is also vital in determining where to look for buyers.

If you do not own all the shares, you need to ensure other shareholders agree on what is for sale (your shares or every shareholder's?). You will also have to consider how you expect to be paid, for example, a cash deal with shares in the new company or a deferred amount. Do not rule out the possibility of a management buy-out, or a financial institution acquiring a minority shareholding and leaving other shareholdings intact. A good corporate finance adviser will go through all of this before you start the process and help you get a clear strategy and objectives.

Whatever your reasons are for a potential sale, ensure that you think about how this process is going to work and what you need in place to achieve this.

2. Timing and tax planning are vital

The best time to sell is when you are not under pressure to do so. This is because you can choose when to put your company on the market. For example, in a seasonal business you would probably want to have made your profits and maximise the sale value before putting it up for sale. Timing the sale to coincide with a newly completed set of audited accounts available is always helpful as this can reduce uncertainty over the profit and assets being sold.

Taxation planning is another essential part of a good exit strategy. It may be worthwhile accelerating the process, or delaying it, in order to take full advantage of the relevant tax reliefs. Capital gains tax legislation will affect company disposals and can be subject to change. Examples like this need to be considered carefully as they are particularly relevant. There may also be ways of structuring a deal to provide you and the vendor with a revenue stream rather than just a capital gain. If the company owns the property it occupies, you should consider whether ownership could be transferred to you to give you an annual rental income.

Planning of this sort gives you greater flexibility in a negotiation. Not every buyer will have unlimited resources and you may be able to extract a higher post-tax return if you can provide a range of options. It is important that your advisers are fully aware of your needs (and priorities) and can discuss technical matters with the purchaser's advisers.

The sale process may take several months. If you are under a time pressure it may detract from your ability to negotiate sensibly and effectively, as well as preventing you from managing the company effectively. This is why planning the realistic timing of a sale is a critical part of any exit strategy. Too often, companies look to sell when they have 'peaked' or the future is uncertain, which will only decrease the value. You should time your exit for when you have exciting growth prospects or good opportunities ahead as these will be what convinces any buyer to complete a deal.

3. Valuing the company

Valuing any company can be a complex process. The easy response to the question how much is my company worth is 'the amount a willing buyer is prepared to pay a willing vendor'.

Before embarking on the sales process, you will need to have a reasonable idea of the company's value. It may be based on net assets, cash generation or a multiple of profits or a combination of these. The rate of improvement or decline in these will also be an influence. Some markets use very specific methods, such as a value per room in the case of hotels, or a percentage of fee income for professional practices. Profits will not always be the sole influence here; it is often about future potential.

Valuing companies is not always straightforward as some of the factors involved may be difficult to quantify. Some of the most common methods of valuation include:

- Net asset value (NAV)

- Multiples of price/earnings (P/E)

- Discounted cash flow (DCF)

- Future return on investment (ROI)

The strategic importance of the company to a third party and future earnings are among other key elements which potential buyers will look at as indicators of its value. So, if you are thinking of selling, you (and your fellow shareholders) should ask yourselves what you would realistically pay for the company if you were entering the market. You should also think about how you would value it in this situation.

Some factors will not always be financial indicators, so consider the value that a buyer might be prepared to pay for the criteria that defines the value. This can be summarised in the following table which you can complete:

Company valuation criteria

Components which make up the value	Actual amount each part could be worth?
Future growth potential	
Other assets (experience of employees, technological advances)	
Current and future sales and profitability	
Nature and strength of customer base	
Strength of products/services compared to main competitors	
Company's reputation and stability in the market	
Any intellectual property (IP)	

Seek professional advice, but make sure it is impartial. It is not unknown for selling agents to indicate an attractive valuation in order to sign up a vendor, so take up references and speak to previous clients.

You need to establish at an early stage your minimum acceptable price and if there are separate elements of it and what is negotiable or worth trading with. For example, you might be prepared to accept a consultancy contract for two years, or use of a vehicle for a defined period in return for a reduced capital sum. In summary, make sure you know what your minimum acceptable price is and do not enter the process unless your advisers are confident that you can achieve it.

4. Grooming the company for sale

In the months or even years before the sale process begins, a thorough look at all aspects of the company is essential. In the interest of boosting profitability think of how:

- Margins can be increased

- Non-business expenses can be reduced

- Expenditure with a long-term payback, such as an advertising campaign, can be deferred

- Longer-term sales contracts can be put in place to give certainty of income

Non-business or surplus assets should be disposed of. Purchasers will not want these so transfer any such assets into private ownership or realise some cash. One way this can be done is by paying a pre-sale dividend or making a pension fund contribution. Both can, in the right circumstances, be a tax-efficient method of receiving part of the sales proceeds.

Look closely at the management structure. If the company is totally dependent on you then many buyers will 'walk away' or want to discount the price to balance their risk. A purchaser will not need to have to draft in a new management team if you can demonstrate that your second-line management is capable of running the company. If you are the business owner, consider the organisational structure of the company.

There are many other matters involved in grooming a company for sale (e.g. taxation, legal reviews). You will need to choose your professional advisers carefully by ensuring that they have previous disposal experience.

5. Consider the alternative exit options

There are several ways for shareholders to realise the value of their investment, depending on the size and nature of the |company, for example:

- A flotation on a recognised Stock Market

- A trade sale

- A management buy-out (MBO)

- A management buy-in (MBI), i.e. a deal involving new management, usually backed by a venture capitalist, combined with the remaining management

- Close the company and sell the assets

Flotation is rarely a realistic option for a business owner wishing to unlock value and sell the company. Generally a company comes on the market on the back of its main directors and, if anything, they are likely to be required to remain locked in at least for the short term. It may be an opportunity to realise some value, but not the entire holding. For those wanting a 'clean' exit, either a trade sale or MBO is the most likely.

6. Prepare a decent sales memorandum

Preparing a sales memorandum (or prospectus) is intended to be a selling document and should show the full potential of the company. Its purpose is to bring a purchaser to the negotiating table. It needs to be an honest document and its contents capable of independent verification. The last thing needed is for a prospective purchaser to find it bears no resemblance to reality.

Presentation is something which needs a strong focus. Product literature, charts and tables are much more relevant than pages and pages of management accounts. Also, clarity of language is more important than technical detail or precision.

You may wish to produce different versions emphasising different attractions, as certain purchasers will have different priorities or objectives. Stress the good points, but don't overlook or hide the bad ones. Put disclaimers on the document, but bear in mind that the due diligence process will find you out if you are trying to conceal something.

You will be aware of any items you'd rather a potential buyer didn't see and you should decide at the outset how and when these will be disclosed. It is preferable to disclose rather than be caught out, otherwise trust will quickly disappear (perhaps along with the purchaser!).

Think of examples of items that should be included in your own sales memorandum, which you can complete in the following way:

Sales memorandum

Sales memorandum items to include	Your own sales memorandum summary
1. The company address, contact details, auditors etc	
2. Who the shareholders are and their stake in the company	
3. The company's products and services and opportunities	
4. Market place and competitor analysis	
5. Key employees and the potential for future growth	
6. A financial overview and the benefits to a potential buyer	
7. Any other factors you think are relevant	

A good sales memorandum will help to make it clear what you are selling. Don't make it too long or too detailed (perhaps a maximum of twenty pages). By doing this you should have a document which focuses on the benefits to a potential buyer. This will make it easier to get the main message across, i.e. to gain interest and set up meetings to progress the sale.

7. Identifying interested parties

The process you have gone through to date may well point the way to a likely buyer profile. If you want cash from a deal it may rule out buyers below a certain size. If you are looking for a purchaser who will safeguard the future employment of all your employees, there is little point talking to known 'asset strippers'.

In conjunction with your professional advisers you should put together a list of possible buyers. You may well have market information about prospective trade buyers, but do not rule out new entrants to the sector. Directors or specialist professional advisers should have the ability to identify 'non-trade' buyers who may be prepared to pay a premium to enter your market.

Consider the most effective option for bringing the sale to the buyer's attention. A private sale has the benefit of keeping confidentiality intact with minimum disruption to relations with customers, suppliers and employees. Advertising that the company is for sale may send out the wrong signals, as well as bringing in potential parties who are not serious or don't have the funds to buy a company. An auction or sealed tender bid can be appropriate when price is the prime differentiating factor between purchasers.

Use advisers to approach potential purchasers and always ask them to sign a confidentiality agreement. This should offer the name of the company in return for the confidentiality. It should be a simple process involving a standardised letter. However, some business sectors (such as pharmaceuticals for example), may require something specifically drafted and may well be better negotiated by your lawyers.

Keep your target list to manageable proportions. Even if you have a long list, prioritise it into smaller segments of ten to twenty targets. That's more than enough to deal with at any one time and if the first twenty say no you may need to rethink!

8. Keep your focus until the transaction is complete

The selling process can be an exciting one, but it is also time consuming. It is easy to have many meetings with prospective purchasers and their advisers. Ideally you will, as part of the grooming for sale process, put a supporting tier of management in place who can deal with day-to-day issues. For a purchaser who is aware that you will be moving on, it is a benefit to know that this is the case. More importantly, it will help ensure that the performance of the company does not suffer.

It is not unknown for the price to be forced down towards the end of protracted negotiations because business performance has suffered and the purchasers realise they are not going to get what was on offer at the outset.

Morale can suffer badly during this period if employees are not kept reasonably informed, or even offered the chance to buy the company. The attitude of your employees will be picked up by the buyer during pre-acquisition contact. No buyer will be particularly keen to take on a demoralised workforce without taking account of it in negotiations. So make a note of this and factor it in to your selling process.

9. Control the deal and negotiate sensibly

When you get to the negotiation stage of a company sale you need to ensure that you don't lose control of events. This applies to vendors, which may make for tougher but perhaps less frustrating negotiations if both sides are professional in their approach.

Don't be flattered by the attention given by prospective buyers. They are not there for your benefit, but theirs. Be objective, especially if they start to talk too much about how good your company is, or if you get an early cash offer. If this happens, take a step back.

Don't spend time with potential buyers who appear to be wasting your time. This can be resolved by asking them to produce evidence of funding at an early stage. Offering a 'lock-out' (exclusive negotiations and access to information for a limited period) for a price will also do this. You should have decided what you want from the deal and have recognised that a certain type of buyer may be prepared to pay a premium price. If the buyer you are dealing with is not offering the deal you want and never looks like doing so, don't accept it. Take the decision to terminate negotiations and remain in control of the selling process.

Consider what buyers are trying to achieve. They want to buy and you want to sell, subject to price etc. Don't get too involved in negotiating if it is obscuring the real objectives. Try to research the buyer's specific needs. A buyer looking for a brand name may be persuaded to take on more debt. One looking for a profit stream may not wish to acquire non-core assets. It is best to pass the really detailed parts which you don't agree on to a professional adviser, with clear instructions as to the desired outcome. This avoids you being seen as difficult and you will come across as assertive and businesslike.

Ultimately you must be prepared to 'walk away' from a business offer. Sometimes this ploy is used for dramatic effect, but if a deal cannot be agreed within your required terms, let this be known clearly and unemotionally and terminate negotiations.